The Psychology of Clergy

The Psychology of Clergy

H. Newton Malony

and

Richard A. Hunt

MOREHOUSE PUBLISHING
Harrisburg, PA

Copyright © H. Newton Malony and Richard A. Hunt 1991

Morehouse Publishing

Editorial Office:

871 Ethan Allen Highway
Suite 204
Ridgefield, CT 06877

Corporate Office:

P.O. Box 1321
Harrisburg, PA 17105

Library of Congress Cataloging-in-Publication Data
Malony, H. Newton,
      The psychology of clergy / H. Newton Malony and Richard A. Hunt.
         p.   c.m.
      Includes bibliographical references and index.
      ISBN 0-8192-1450-7 (pbk.)
      1. Clergy—Psychology.   I. Hunt, Richard A., 1931-
II. Title.
BV4398.M35 1991   91-28083
253'.2—dc20   CIP

Printed in the United States of America
by BSC LITHO
Harrisburg, PA 17105

Contents

Introduction

"Don't push me!" How many times have we heard children say this to their parents? Nobody likes to be pushed. Being pushed means "being forced; not being in control." No one of us likes to be forced. No one of us likes to lose control. We want to be in charge of our lives. We want to feel that we can make our own decisions.

This book is about the "push" of ordained, professional ministry. Clergypersons are classic examples of people who feel "pushed around." Often, clergy report they feel their lives are out of control. As one rabbi stated, "I am jerked here and there by the expectations of the congregation and the routine demands of the job; my life is not my own." And the dean of a cathedral commented, "I am not doing what I was trained to do—it's as simple as that!"

Some clergy may enjoy being pushed, but they are few and far between. The general disenchantment, the disillusionment, the discouragement, the disinterest, and the despair that characterize the functioning of many ministers is a direct result of not wanting be pushed *but* not knowing what to do about it.

Being *pulled* by goals is a thousand times better than being pushed by expectations. That is what this book is all about. In fact, the book might have been titled "How to Turn Pushes into Pulls." Clergy who are pulled by their own goals have energy, enthusiasm, excitement, and inspiration. They have insight into who they are, what they do, and why they function the way they do. They know what they want and how to get it.

This book is also about "consciousness raising," to borrow a term from the women's movement. Knowledge is power. Clergy must obtain some new knowledge if they are to gain power over their lives. What clergy don't know *will* hurt them, to turn a phrase. We hope this book will raise the self-awareness of clergy to a new level.

Of course, new information by itself will not change pushes into pulls. Clergy will need to take the newly-acquired knowledge and act on it. Insight based on new information is the beginning, even if it is not the end, of change. This book about the psychology of clergy is intended to serve as a starting place for helping ministers begin the journey from push to pull.

A bit of history is in order. Being a clergyperson is old. The *study* of clergy is new. As early as the fourteenth chapter of the Book of Genesis, a reference is made to a "priest of God Most High" (14:18). Very soon after God called Abraham to be the father of the Hebrew nation, a person called "priest" was set aside to do religious work. The first several books of the Bible contain many assertions about and prescriptions for priests. In contemporary terms, we could say that Scripture speaks about vocational choice (the sons of Aaron are to be priests, Exod. 28:1), about job descriptions (what priests are to do, Lev. 4:1ff), and about personality characteristics (priests are to be holy, Lev. 21:7). Many writings of the eighth-century prophets refer to job evaluations of priests ("I hate, I despise your feasts and I take no delight in your solemn assemblies. . . . But let justice roll down like waters and righteousness like an everflowing stream" Amos 5:21-24). Furthermore, the writer of Timothy details the job qualifications for clergy in his list of characteristics for "anyone who aspires to the office of bishop" (1 Tim. 3:1-7).

While clergy have often featured in the world's literature, the *study* of professional clergy is much newer than any of those writings. By *study* is meant the kind of analyses and interpretations that emerge from the work of sociologists and psychologists, and theirs are very young disciplines—less than two hundred years old at best.

What is it that these "social/behavioral" sciences do? They study people with the same rigor that the older sciences study nature. What the human sciences lack in age, they have made up for in quantity! Human behavior has been studied ad nauseam! Investigations have ranged from depth perception of the eye to the psychodynamics of dreams; from the nature of group interaction to the effects of social class on voting preferences; from the comparison of child-rearing practices across cultures to the stimulation of pleasure centers in the brain. This broad span of research has been no less true of the study of clergypersons.

This book is about those studies. The title is a bit misleading, however. The term *psychology* may be used in a broad sense to refer to all those fields that study human beings. This includes sociology and anthropology as well as organizational, vocational, developmental, social, and personnel psychology. In this volume, *psychology* is used in a narrow sense in that it focuses on the experience and behavior of the individual clergyperson. The book is intended as a manual to which clergy can refer in order to understand themselves better. The material is less a general discussion of the place of clergy in the wider culture and more a review of what is known about the role of clergy in specific situations. It is also narrow in that it focuses on the experience of "parish" clergy in contrast to specialized roles such as that of Father Andrew Greeley, the novelist who, although he considers himself primarily a priest, is nevertheless not involved in the weekly administration of a local church. This book is written to those clergy who run synagogues, shepherd committees, preach sermons, administer sacraments, teach Scripture, counsel parishioners, and conduct funerals.

Another qualification should also be made. This book is about clergy in the Western world. More specifically, it is about clergy in the United States. No attempt is made to compare or contrast these conclusions with what could be said about the role of clergy in societies to the east or to the west of the United States. This does not mean that such comparisons, or even evaluations, of clergy across cultures are not needed. They are. But that is not the intent of this volume. Perhaps a book such as this could be considered one of the foundation stones on which those kinds of studies could be made. This does not mean that the ideas presented here will be offered in a noncritical or imperialistic way—as if clergy in the United States are better than those in other lands. Some judgments will be made, but they will be intracultural rather than cross-cultural evaluations. The majority of clergy to whom this book is written must learn to function more effectively in this culture rather than some other.

We hope psychologists and sociologists have learned something of value about clergy in the last two centuries. More often than not the efforts have been inductive rather than idealistic. Inductive means the studies have been based on observations of what clergy do and how they behave rather than on what they *should* do or how they *should* behave. This does not mean the studies have been devoid of ideals or values. The very fact that clergy have so often been the subject of investigations attests to the value scholars place on their role in society.

Being inductive instead of idealistic implies that students of human behavior see clergy through a clear lens; they do not put on rose-colored glasses to look at "religious" professionals. They take clergy as they are. They observe clergy behavior as human behavior and clergy themselves as no less, and no more, than human beings. In a sense, this adds dignity to the results of their endeavors.

We hope that these essays will assist in dignifying the profession of ministry. Although knowing what being a clergyperson is like from the viewpoint of psychology can tell us much, it, too, has its limitations. Being inductive and descriptive is a strength that is also a weakness. Filling an important role in society may be enough for the social/behavioral scientist, but that will not be sufficient as a "reason for being" among clergy themselves. Ultimately, purpose for ministry must come from *outside* the types of studies reported here. Furthermore, research is always based on limited samples, and that, too, is both a strength and a weakness. Research conclusions are based on inferences gleaned from selected groups of people. Many clergy are never surveyed. Rules have exceptions; data should not tyrannize us. Each clergyperson is unique and may well be the one who does not fit the results. Averages are no more than that—averages.

A statement by Erik Erikson encompasses all the themes included in this book. He contends that the ego crisis of late adulthood is one of "despair versus integrity." It is crucial that those involved in ministry as a vocation live their lives with integrity rather than despair. The goal of this volume could easily be stated in Erikson's words. He defined *integrity* in this way:

> It is the acceptance of one's one and only life cycle as something that had to be and that, by necessity, permitted of no substitutions: it thus means a new, a different love of one's parents. It is a comradeship with the ordering ways of distant times and different pursuits, as expressed in the simple products and sayings of such times and pursuits. Although aware of the relativity of all the various life styles which have given meaning to human striving, the possessor of integrity is ready to defend the dignity of his own life style against all physical and economic threats. For he knows that an individual life is the accidental coincidence of but one life cycle with but one segment of history; and that for him all human integrity stands or falls with the one style of integrity of which he partakes. . . ."[1]

Chapter 1.
Ministry:
A Unique Position

Clergy play a distinctive role in life. They occupy a unique position in our society. The following examples illustrate the not-so-subtle ways in which ministry differs from other vocations.

On a cool Monday morning, Hugh sat in the breakfast nook just off his kitchen drinking coffee while reading the newspaper. He served as pastor of Immanuel Lutheran Church, located just across the parking lot from his home. Monday meant vacation—his day off. Glancing up from the newspaper, Hugh watched several cars pass along the street. "People on their way to work," he mused. He waved to the driver of one car—the chairperson of the church ushers, who worked in production at a nearby aluminum plant.

Yes, on Monday, his day off, Hugh would not go to work as did most of his parishioners and other employed people. For a few minutes he thought about his life as a minister. "I wonder how it would feel to have the weekend off?" he asked himself. Of course, this was not a new thought. Hugh had often compared himself to the average person. He not only worked weekends, he was involved in church work several evenings each week when most other people were home. His plans for study did not always work out because of interruptions. Sickness, family emergencies, special meetings, counseling, and other needs of members of his congregation regularly required his attention. He kept a hectic pace—sometimes working eighty hours a week. "Running a church must surely be different from running a business," he thought.

On the Saturday afternoon prior to Hugh's Monday morning reflections, Sally, wife of William Gaylor, the pastor of Northside Baptist Assembly, called upstairs to her husband. "Bill, will you

1

please hurry. We'll be late to the Willing Workers picnic." As Bill
dried off from a shower, he thought about the demands of the day.
He had spent the morning in his study finishing the sermon he
planned to preach the next day. After lunch he had visited a new
mother in the hospital and then mowed the front yard grass. And
now an expected appearance at another church function required
additional time and effort.

He really didn't want to go to the picnic. This would be the third
Saturday in a row that he and his wife had spent significant time at
some Sunday school class social. As the pastor, he knew he must
go. The members expected him to attend. "I never get to do
anything with my friends," he exclaimed aloud. And then he
thought, "If I did, some of the other church members would be
jealous. A minister just can't win," he concluded. His mind then
turned to the sermon. "In what other occupation is a leader
expected to go on a picnic with people one day and preach to
them the next?" he asked himself. Bill finished dressing, walked
slowly down the stairs, and called to his wife, "I'm ready, Sally.
Let's go."

Hugh's and Bill's situations illustrate only a few of the distinctive
features of clergy life. Clergy do not have the weekend off. They
have little control over their schedules. They work long hours.
They preach to those with whom they socialize. Their entertainment is often limited to church socials. These characteristics,
by themselves, do not make ministry absolutely different from
other vocations. After all, other people work on Sunday, too! In
combination with a number of other factors, however, these form
a picture of an occupation that is, at the very least, unusual. This
chapter is directed to an exploration of ministry's uniqueness.

Historical Changes in Ministerial Stereotypes

Historian Brooks Holifield suggests that the stereotype of the
ideal minister has tended to be a reflection of society's image of
the cultural "hero."[1] Several images have dominated the outlook
toward ministers during the last two centuries. These still influence the picture of ministry today.

Frontier revivalists became the embodiment of the "common
man." They illustrated the best democratic virtues: enthusiasm,
friendliness, and commitment. Whereas intellect and doctrinal
purity were considered aristocratic, feeling and will were capac-
ities available to every person. Although other professionals, such
as lawyers and doctors, functioned out of special knowledge and

skill, frontier preachers interacted with everyone through their warmth and courageous affirmation of virtue. They depended on their personality, not on their intellectual brilliance. This image of the minister centered on morality and cordiality rather than intellect or sacramental office. Folksiness, friendliness, religious feeling, and conviction were the stock-in-trade for effective colonial ministry. Jonathan Edwards probably epitomized this clergy image.

Alongside the image of the minister as the common man, however, there grew up the image of the minister as "gentleman." The American hero in the early part of the nineteenth century, as seen in secular magazines, shifted from the rough-hewn frontiersman to that of the refined and learned gentleman. Holifield noted that, by the late 1820, books were being written about the manners and etiquette of clergy—all of which paralleled society's growing admiration for "gentlemanly" behavior. As church members became more urbanized, they began to prefer cultured and refined ministers. People who settled in towns and cities were not comfortable with folksy revivalists. Urban clergy were expected to exemplify the best in manners and dress. Whereas the image of the clergy as populists was based on their personality, the image of the clergy as gentlemen was based on reputation.

The dominant image of the cultural hero changed again after the Civil War. During this time of great economic expansion, the picture of the hero as a "refined gentleman" gave way to the image of the hero as a "man of power." Vision, forcefulness, the ability to persuade the masses, and fame were admired characteristics. Preachers such as Henry Ward Beecher, who preached to over three thousand persons with brilliance and charm, dominated the scene. Revivalists such as Dwight L. Moody and Billy Sunday also exemplified the ideal. Instead of neighborly personality or gentlemanly reputation, clergy were judged powerful by the number of people they were able to influence.

However, disillusionment with the ruthlessness of industrial monarchs toward the end of the nineteenth century provoked a new hero, the "liberal progressive." Admired ministers were judged not so much by their power as by their social consciousness, their moral purpose, and their high ideals, according to Holifield. Washington Gladden embodied this image. The social gospel became the norm. Reformers became the most admired clergy. In addition to being able to preach, these ministers became active in politics, union movements, slum clearance, and other efforts. Instead of personality, reputation, or power, a concern for social justice became the quality that exemplified ideal clergy during this period.

After the First World War, however, this concern for social reform faded, and admiration for those capable of motivating and mobilizing the nation for battle came to the fore. The cultural hero became the one who could manage a bureaucratic organization effectively. Ministry felt the effects of the new science of management. Church administration grew in importance. Efficiency and effectiveness dominated the standards by which to judge ministry. Experience replaced personality, reputation, power, or social concern as the most admired quality in clergy.

These images (the populist, the gentleman, the achiever, the reformer, and the manager) continue to inform the picture of ministry today. Add two other features, the spiritual and the sacramental, and one has a complete list of the conflicting standards of ministry in contemporary society.

By "spiritual" is meant the persistent concern throughout almost all historical periods with the personal spiritual life of clergy. Ministers who evidence a contact with the transcendent and who practice holy habits have always been esteemed. In most every age, ministers have been expected to embody what they preach. The word *parson*, which applied to the Puritan preacher, was no accident. It referred to the one who lived in the house (parsonage) provided by a church and expressed the fact that people in the community wanted to have confidence that this clergyperson (the parson) would act and be religious. In a sense, clergy have been judged by how they lived, as much as by their experience, personality, power, skill, and social concern. In more charismatic circles, this has included the ability to express certain spiritual gifts, such as discernment, healing, and speaking in tongues—all of which were thought to be evidence of a minister's contact with the divine.

The "sacramental" dimension refers to the ability of ministers to skillfully perform the unique tasks of ministry (i.e., teach the Scriptures, preach effectively, administer the sacraments, and celebrate the eucharist). Those who have done these well have been admired. The emphasis here has been less on the persuasiveness of ministers and more on their faithfulness to doctrine and their ability to functionally relate faith to life and provide the ordinances of the church meaningfully at critical moments. These duties have been called the charter roles of ministry in that they were considered the original tasks required of clergy from the beginning of the church. Thus, clergy have been judged by how well they fulfilled their official duties alongside their manners, social concern, managerial skills, and personalities.

The Current Picture of Clergy Uniqueness

Sociologist Jackson Carroll discusses the current state of clergy uniqueness in a manner that incorporates the ideal clergy images emergent during the last two centuries.[2] He suggests that the present picture no longer depends primarily on personal qualities. Instead, clergy are judged on how technically expert they are, how spiritually they act, and how much official authority they have. The diagram below depicts these dimensions. Carroll's diagram shows four clergy models.

Four Types of Clergy Authority

		Bases of Authority	
		Sacred	Expert
	Person	Type A	Type D
Degree of Institutionalization			
	Office	Type B	Type C

Type A. Sacred Authority, Person Institutionalization

Type A clergy rely on the spiritual image of ministry almost entirely. They understand their authority to be grounded in their possession of spiritual gifts that validate their claim to having been called into ministry. Their sense of themselves is that to be a minister means to exhibit the gifts of healing, prophecy, evangelism, prayer, devotion, and other spiritual gifts, or else they are not authentic. In a sense, this type of minister depends heavily on personality and reputation, but the emphasis is not on manners or social skills as much as on spiritual qualities. Although this type of clergyperson appears in all denominations, it is especially represented in the charismatic and Pentecostal traditions.

The authority of Type A clergy is based on their possession of contact with the sacred rather than on expertise in skills and such as administration or persuasion. They take no pride in their ordination as minister or their selection as pastor of a church. The institution of the church is not nearly as important to them as their personal ability to demonstrate that they are in communion with the divine and that they have been given special abilities by God.

Type B. Sacred Authority, Office Institutionalization

Type B clergy also rely on their ability to perform certain sacred duties, but this ability is not dependent as much on their personal qualities as it is on the church's choice of them to do these tasks. This does not mean their personal lives are unimportant, but it does imply that the performance of certain duties, such as celebration of the eucharist and preaching, are not an expression of character but of ordination. The Roman Catholic Church long ago concluded that the efficacy of the sacrament is not dependent on the character of the priest.

Nevertheless, office and person are not radically separate in this model—as can be seen by the attention paid in Roman Catholicism, for example, to the socialization of priests. This type of clergy see themselves as representatives of God through the sacramental-liturgical roles to which the church has ordained them. Here, ordination by the church permits them to perform these duties. Parishioners submit to their authority because of the office they hold. Although this type of clergy can be seen throughout Christendom, they are especially prevalent in the Episcopal, Orthodox, and Roman Catholic traditions.

Type C. Expert Authority, Office Institutionalization

Type C clergy gain their authority from their expertise in the performance of official duties. Less emphasis is placed on whether one performs a sacred task (as in the sacraments) or exhibits certain qualities (as in spiritual gifts), and more emphasis is placed on how well one knows and communicates a given denominational tradition (as in Presbyterianism). John Calvin, in fact, institutionalized this model by calling the minister the "teaching elder."

Neither manners nor personality matter to this type of clergy as much as knowledge of Scripture and tradition, coupled with the ability to communicate and persuade. Preaching and teaching become the emphasized tasks. Being an expert in these matters is less a personal quality or an ordained responsibility and more a demonstrated skill. This clergy type is probably represented in the performance of organizational tasks as well as duties related to a given theological tradition. While this type of clergy can be seen in all denominations, it is most prevalent in churches within the Reformed tradition. In some ways, their persuasive power reminds one of the achieving ministers of the late nineteenth century.

Type D. Expert Authority, Person Institutionalization

Type D clergy are most similar to populist ministers of the early nineteenth century as well as to the gentleman clergy who followed. They also evidence some of the qualities of the managerial clergy who came to the fore after the First World War. While demonstrating expertise in the personal skills that go into making a good presentation of themselves, they are also influential because of their personality and social skills, which are only indirectly related to such official duties as preaching and worship leadership.

This type of clergyperson impresses others and knows how to lead effectively because of a winning "style." Type D clergy evoke cohesion. Their performance is approved because of their informal expertise in interpersonal relations. They are probably equally well represented in all denominations. Studies suggest that across traditions in contemporary America, personal skills of this kind are highly regarded.

In summary, these four types combine the images of populist, gentleman, achiever, reformer, organizer, charismatic, and celebrant that have dominated the picture of ministers over the last two hundred years. As can be seen in the preceding discussion, the uniqueness of clergy in our society is dependent upon the priority clergy and their churches have given to sacred—in contrast to expert—skills and the extent to which these skills are evident in personal living as distinct from official duties.

Clergy Authority: Grounded in the Church

In each of the types, the ability of clergy to function is due to an interaction between the expectations of the church and the ability of the clergy to meet those expectations. Where the fit has been a good one, the clergy have been accorded authority. Where the fit has been bad, the clergy have lost this power. Both Hugh and William, in the illustrations with which this chapter began, evidenced a mixture of satisfaction and dissatisfaction with the demands of their positions.

Authority refers to the type of influence one has over others. For clergy to survive, they must have authority. The position that clergy occupy is dependent upon the willingness of people to support their role and follow their leadership. Carroll defines authority as "legitimate power" in the sense that influence over others is considered acceptable because people perceive what the leader is doing as for their good.[3]

Understanding this relationship between what people feel their needs are and their perception of how well leaders meet their expectations is essential in order to adequately comprehend the uniqueness of ministry in today's world. In each case discussed above, a group of people (i.e., a church) believes that a certain type of minister will meet their needs better than another type. The extent to which a given clergyperson does, in fact, meet these expectations is the extent to which members of a congregation will allow that minister to influence them.

This means that ministry, as opposed to almost any other profession, is dependent upon an institution, the church. While all vocations require customers who will buy their product, ministry has no independent existence apart from those "customers," as does medicine, law, teaching, and other professions. This fact has led many to question whether clergy can be called "professionals." Although the possibility that clergy are not professionals seems ludicrous—in light of the tradition that refers to theology, medicine, and law as the "three oldest professions"—the criteria for being professional are difficult for clergy to meet.

Clergy: Professionals or Bureaucrats?

For a vocation to be called a "profession," several criteria must be met. Ministry may meet some of these but not others. First, for the practice of a skill to be referred to and accepted as a profession means "to have something to profess." Clergy have no problem with this requirement because they profess the Christian gospel. The gospel is to clergy what medicine is to physicians and the law is to attorneys. Professions have a body of knowledge they possess and in which they are the experts. Clergy are professionals in religion. They are considered the experts in this area.

Second, for the practice of a skill to be referred to and accepted as a profession means to offer one's knowledge to the public. Clergy meet this requirement, too. They are public figures, and they offer religion "for sale" in the same manner that a physician offers healing and a lawyer provides advice to the public regarding legal matters. This comparison may seem crass, but it is nevertheless true: clergy are the representatives of a product offered for public sale.

The third requirement in order for the practice of a skill to be referred to and accepted as a profession is more difficult for clergy to meet. To be a professional means to offer one's knowledge to the public independently. Parish clergy do not do this in the same manner as physicians or attorneys. Ministers do not function independently. They do not establish offices, put their names on lobby directories in public buildings, charge fees for services, or advertise in the yellow pages. Clergy work for churches, not for themselves. Although recognized by each state to practice religion, as in performing weddings and conducting funerals, they are not licensed. They are ordained by churches to serve as pastors and priests. Clergy are not independent of the churches they serve. Even pastoral counselors, as understood by the American Association of Pastoral Counselors, must be endorsed by a denomination and must remain responsible to a church body even though they function in freestanding offices.

Perhaps a better term for ministers would be *servant bureaucrats*, rather than professionals. They are servants of the gospel and of the church. They are middle-level managers, or bureaucrats, in the best sense of the word. They do not create their product, the gospel, but they are given the task of applying it to life and enabling the members of churches to live out their faith as the Body of Christ in the world. They serve God, and they serve people in, essentially, an organizational role. Theirs is not a profession so much as it is a calling.

Ministry: A Calling

In writing about the uniqueness of ministry, Thomas Gannon suggests that ministry was more a calling than a profession.[4] When commenting on the first requirement for being a profession (i.e., a body of knowledge), Gannon notes that clergy lack "a clearly defined technical body of knowledge that can be applied to the solution of technical problems."[5] Unlike doctors or lawyers, ministers cannot practice their profession; they must live it.

Gannon notes that the knowledge possessed by clergy is not the kind that controls events. Rather, ministers give meaning to events, and they exemplify as well as represent that meaning. Pastors invite people into a community of interpretation in which all of life is given a new meaning. They do not possess this knowledge as a set of techniques for solving problems but as a way of life that they attempt to model. Instead of presenting themselves as masters of a set of ideas and tools, clergy present themselves as having answered a moral obligation to represent an understanding of life based on the Christian revelation.

Thus, the question most committees assessing candidates for ministry ask ("Have you had a call to ministry?") is essentially appropriate. Ministry is a calling to the role of servant bureaucrat.

Labeling clergy as "those who are called to servant bureaucracy" is a way of doing justice to the fact that there is no ministerial vocation apart from the church. It also does honor to the unique manner in which ministry is a role that must be lived as well as expressed.

The Monday morning and Saturday afternoon experiences of

Hugh and Bill, with which this chapter began, only scratched the surface of the ways in which clergy play a unique role in our society. Perhaps this chapter has illumined other ways in which cultural expectations, historical accidents, institutional warrants, and personal responses to the transcendent all intermix to make the position of clergy essentially different from the many other vocations in style, approach, and purpose.

Chapter 2.
Why People
Enter Ministry

Have you ever looked at a group picture of lawyers or teachers or physicians or accountants? While looking at the photo, did you fantasize that you noticed some distinctive characteristic distinguishing one group from another—only to be disappointed because they all looked so much alike? Every group had short, tall, sober, jovial, attractive, ugly, rotund, and thin individuals. In fact, in suits and dresses each group looked like a gathering of bankers!

You probably would have the same experience if a group photo of ministers was added to the assemblage. You would be unable to tell the ministers from the accountants, lawyers, physicians, or teachers. There would be more differences *within* each group than *between* them.

What determines who enters the ministry and who does not? Is it all happenstance? Is the choice of clergy as a profession a function of environmental accident? Are there no features that distinguish clergy from other people? Are there no characteristics that determine, in part, who will enter a religious vocation?

Answering these questions is important for people considering ministry, as well as for those wondering if they made the right choice. When looking at a picture of clergy, it is one thing to say, "It looks as if God calls all kinds of people into ministry," and quite another to remark, "Anybody can be a minister." While not implying that it would be best if all ministers were carbon copies of each other, some features characterize many, if not most, clergy.

Circumstance or Personality?

In looking at the reasons why individuals choose ministry as a profession, it is helpful to differentiate between *circumstance* and *personality*. Circumstance involves outside-the-person traits. On the one hand, circumstances may awaken interests people did not

11

realize they had prior to a particular experience. On the other hand, personality traits may motivate individuals to seek certain activities and experience. The question to ask clergy is, "Are you a minister because of unique circumstances or because of certain personality traits?"

For clergy, the usual answer to this question is, "Both." Consider the following two examples. It is almost impossible to separate personality from circumstance in the choices these people made.

Michael had spent a decade as a successful investment banker when he decided to enter the Episcopal priesthood. After serving as a vestryman in his medium-size parish for a number of years, he completed a term as senior warden. When their oldest child, Martha, was a junior in high school, he and his wife had taken a turn as youth counselors at the church they all attended.

He had enjoyed each of these responsibilities and, over the past year, had stopped by the church frequently just to talk with the rector and inquire if he could assist in some way. Occasionally he had accompanied the rector on hospital calls and had taken the sacrament to several shut-ins.

Increasingly, during daily rides on the elevated train into the Loop of downtown Chicago, Michael thought about what serving as a priest might be like. Finally, just before lunch one day, he called the bishop and asked for an appointment. The bishop had many questions: "Do you realize you will need to go to seminary for three years? Does your wife approve of this career change: What will your teenage son and daughter think? Are you aware that priesthood pays far less than investment banking?"

Michael satisfied the bishop with his answers. After working through the issues with his family and completing seminary, he became the rector of a parish in Minneapolis. Was his decision to become a clergyperson due to personality or circumstance? Probably both.

David, an Evangelical Lutheran Church pastor in New Orleans, decided to enter ministry at a summer youth camp while in his midteens. In his denomination in the 1950s, a persuasive preacher customarily spoke each evening during camp. These speakers usually ended their sermons by giving the audience an opportunity to make a decision. One night the preacher asked those who wanted to enter "full-time Christian service" to stand.

David's girlfriend stood. He did not know that she had even thought about such a step. When she stood, he felt deeply moved, and goose pimples rose on his arms and neck. He suddenly thought, "If she's willing to do that, why shouldn't I do the same?" He didn't stand but left the meeting in deep thought.

Later that night he told an older friend, "I think God is calling me to become a minister." "Think about it; sleep on it," his friend advised. David took a long walk; he then went to bed. The next morning he met his friend at breakfast. "I still think it's true; I've decided I want to be a pastor," David said.

He finished high school, completed college, graduated from seminary, and became a Lutheran pastor. Sometimes he thinks about the decision he made at summer camp almost thirty-five years ago. He has had a good ministry and enjoys almost every aspect of his job. He wonders what determined his decision. Was it due to his personality or the circumstance of his life at the time? We suspect it was both.

Circumstance

Consider circumstance in more detail. It is not enough to say that David's decision was due to the need in adolescence to make a vocational decision. Although, in Western culture, it is true that adolescence is the time when a person moves from childhood to adulthood, it is also true that vocational choices can legitimately be made much later in life, as Michael's case illustrates. Nevertheless, David was in fact primed by culture and maturation to make a decision. People had asked him, "What are you going to do when you grow up?" Although he admired his pastor, and they were good friends, David had thought of becoming a lawyer or perhaps a businessperson. Ministry had never entered his mind—in spite of the fact that he was very active in his church's youth group and had participated in many parish projects.

One might say, in David's case, that all conditions were ripe for him and that the evening sermon at camp, combined with the shock of seeing his girlfriend stand, was the circumstantial catalyst that made his decision possible.

Erik Erikson, in his book *Young Man Luther*, adds another issue to this discussion of circumstance.[1] He suggests that decisions to enter specific vocations do not come "out of the blue." Youth can enter only one of the occupations available to them *in their culture*.

For example, if one's culture does not provide, among its possible vocations, the role of "Indian chief," it will not be possible for a person to become an Indian chief. In David's case, becoming a Lutheran pastor *was* an option in the culture in which he lived.

His decision to "answer God's call" was channeled through that option. He could not have become a Lutheran pastor in Tibetan or Eskimo culture. This is also true of Michael. No matter what time of life a person makes such a decision, becoming a clergyperson is possible only in a culture that has clergy. In this sense, circumstance is a powerful determinant.

However, Erikson meets a challenge in his own book. Was the role of "Lutheran pastor" available to Martin Luther? Of course, this is a moot question because Luther was the founder of the movement that made it possible for people like David to become Lutheran pastors. But this is just the point: Martin Luther was not a child of circumstance. By nailing his Ninety-five Theses to the church door at Wittenberg, he launched into uncharted territory. He had no idea that another job awaited him outside the Roman Catholic Church. By his actions, he created his own role!

Neither the Luthers nor other entrepreneurs know exactly what the future holds. They boldly carve out new roles for themselves —roles that did not exist prior to their coming on the scene. People are, therefore, not absolutely confined vocationally to the roles provided by their society. Nevertheless, as many have suggested, Luther probably would not have succeeded if not for the German princes who were ready to revolt against Rome and willing to support him.

This does not answer the question of why some people, in the same culture, at the same period in their lives, and exposed to the same experiences, decide to become clergy while others do not. The answer lies in the issues of personality. Let us now consider these issues.

Personality

As noted above, *personality* refers to those inside-the-person traits that supposedly determine an individual's behavior. These traits can be divided into two kinds: feelings and interests. *Feelings* are those inner senses about oneself ranging from guilt to power. Certainly, David exemplified the latter. He felt powerful enough to give himself to the clergy role. He did not enter ministry out of feelings of guilt but from a sense of "call" by God to use his talents in the pastoral role. He did not plead unworthiness, as did Moses when God first called him. Instead, David responded out of a strong conviction that God needed good, strong pastors—and he could be one. *Interests* are those inner inclinations to like certain things and dislike others. Michael exemplifies this. Increasingly, he enjoyed church work. He liked doing what ministers do. He put church activities ahead of other experiences such as sports or hobbies. Clearly, David and Michael appear to have unique features to their personalities. The question is, Is there a type of personality that distinguishes most ministers from other people? Are Michael and David unique or are they exceptions to the rule? A number of studies have attempted to answer these questions.

Feelings

Allen Nauss summarized a number of these investigations in an article entitled "The Ministerial Personality: Myth or Reality."[2] The studies concluded that some negative and some positive traits seemed to characterize clergy. On the basis of the Minnesota Multiphasic Personality Inventory (MMPI), results of some studies showed that ministers tended to be more guilt-ridden, anxious, self-punishing in the face of hostility and aggression, more insecure, defensive, passive, conforming, dependent, rebellious, and idealistic than other people. Add to this list the common presumption, stemming from the latter nineteenth century, that clergy tended to have problems in sexual identity leading to a greater incidence of homosexuality, and one has quite a negative picture of clergy personality traits!

Other studies suggest a far more positive outlook, however. On the basis of other MMPI surveys, clergy have been found to be more self-confident, have higher ego strength, evidence better personal adjustment, show less anxiety, have stronger service interests, and be more creative thinkers than the average person. Results from other measures picture clergy as more gregarious, extroverted, reflective, thoughtful, introspective, nurturant, and venturesome than the average individual.

The Myers-Briggs Type Inventory is used widely in selecting candidates for ministry.[3] It gives easy-to-understand indicators of whether an individual is introverted or extroverted, uses thinking or feeling types of behavior in dealing with life experiences, and so forth. Studies conducted by using this research instrument indicate a tendency for clergy to be extroverted/feeling types of people. This accords with the results from other evaluations that picture clergy as people-oriented, sensitive, and sociable.

Another factor with regard to clergy personality has been the consideration during the past twenty-five years of the rise in the number of women entering ministry. Are their personalities similar to the men who have been surveyed in the past?

One study of seminarians of both sexes found more similarities between women and men candidates for ministry than between female and male graduate education students.[4] Likewise, they were more similar to each other than they were to college graduates of their own sex. They measured high on the need to give and receive nurture as well as the need to be accepted; they were low on the need to be independent and autonomous. Women, in addition, were high on the need for friendships and the need to be dominant but low on the need for being aggressive and the need for change.

Some of these positive characteristics are in contradiction to the negative features noted earlier. "Anxiety" is a good example. One case reported it as above average; another reported it as below average. Clearly the picture is complex, and one would not expect all these features to be present in every minister. One should also remember that most of these studies assessed seminary students on their way to becoming ministers rather than people active as parish clergy.

In regard to negative personality traits such as guilt-proneness, hostility, insecurity, and other characteristics noted above in the MMPI studies, it would be interesting to know whether being in ministry tends to reduce these tendencies. Nauss reported one study in which assessment of Lutheran clergy showed little change in the MMPI profiles that they had taken during seminary some years earlier.

There may be, however, an interaction between personal problems and the extent to which clergy continue to exhibit these traits—as can be seen in another study in which ministers who were more aggressive, more assertive, joyful, strong, and confident reported fewer problems.[5] Whether having fewer problems caused these clergy to exhibit these positive qualities or vice versa is difficult to determine.

It stands to reason, however, that ministry may be one of those vocations to which people are attracted as a means of dealing with some of their problems. Religion affords answers to personal concerns, and perhaps clergy resolve some of their issues through faith and then pass those solutions on to others through their profession. As 1 John 4:19 suggests, "We love because he first loved us!" This may be profoundly true for clerics.

On the other hand, research by R.J. Menges and James E. Dittes concluded some years ago that the clergy role affords people a chance for assertiveness without intimacy.[6] They suggested that many clergy want to relate to others but in a somewhat distant, directive, authoritarian manner. The pulpit and the sermon make this possible by allowing the individual to relate in a highly stylized, controlled, noninteractive manner. The pulpit serves as a barrier to intimacy.

These last observations, although somewhat cynical, may be related to the fact that many clergypersons have suffered loss because of their father's early death and often have been reared by a domineering well-intentioned mother. These mothers pass on to their children an overconcern for ethics, a strong desire to help others, and a preoccupation with maintaining emotional distance.

Interests

It is difficult to distinguish *feeling* traits from *interest* traits. This can be seen most clearly in the comments about clergy extroversion and concern for people. Social interest has been the dominant characteristic to look for in evaluating candidates for ministry. On measures of vocational interests, such as the Strong Vocational Interest Blank, ministerial candidates tend to score high on social interests as compared with the interests of the general population.

Whatever else may be true of clergy, enjoyment of being around people is perhaps the most dominant trait characterizing the profession. The minister who does not like people is a rare exception to the norm. A confirmation of this social interest was reported in a study by J.J. Fabry.[7] Employing Holland's widely used sixfold breakdown of vocational interests into realistic, investigative, social, conventional, enterprising, and artistic areas, he found that ministers tended to rate their attraction to social interaction over twice as high as any other one of the areas. The normative pattern of ranking or all six areas was, from high to low, as follows: social, artistic, investigative, enterprising, realistic, and conventional.

The picture from such a study is that the average clergyperson is gregarious, likes people, enjoys working in groups, is attracted to experiences where she or he can use creative talents, likes to be be innovative, enjoys thinking and theorizing, and prefers tasks that require thinking through assumptions and implications.

Furthermore, the average minister probably would rather work in an institution instead of starting a new organization, likes to work with people or ideas rather than with his or her hands, and finds it very difficult to fit into traditional, dependent tasks where orders are given and rules obeyed.

If, however, one thinks back to Michael, the Episcopal priest who left banking for ministry, it becomes apparent that his preferences were much more specific than a general interest in people. He was interested in a variety of activities that could best be subsumed under the title "religious." He wanted involvement in the lives of people *through* activities of the church: visiting the sick, serving the eucharist, teaching Bible study classes, working with people in crisis, leading youth retreats, and discussing the meaning of life. These are uniquely religious activities.

One of the ways that interest in these uniquely religious tasks has been assessed is through a scale called the Inventory of Religious Activities and Interests, developed by Sam C. Webb working with Samuel Blizzard.[8] This test is a list of 120 things that clergy do in parish ministry. Clergy are asked to rate these activities in terms of how much they enjoy doing them.

These activities, grouped under ten roles in which parish clergy typically work, involve the following: counseling, administration, teaching, studying, evangelizing, spiritually guiding, preaching, reforming, leading worship, and engaging in church music or drama.

As might be expected, there are denominational differences in the preferences that certain clergy have for participating in one role over another. Michael, if he is a typical Episcopal priest, would rate worship leadership higher than evangelizing, while the reverse would be true for a typical Southern Baptist minister.

Without doubt, most people choose ministry because of an interest in doing what ministers do. One noteworthy observation regarding candidates who take the Inventory of Religious Activities and Interests test is that they would greatly enjoy doing almost all the tasks of ministry.

Usually, this is a bit idealistic. Many of these individuals have little or no experience in doing these tasks. At best, they have done them as lay helpers. They tend to romanticize the responsibilities of ministry. After some years in the pastorate, their ratings are not so high. While they continue to enjoy some tasks of ministry, they no longer enjoy others. This is as one would expect. Interests become more differentiated over time. Experience and ability change one's perceptions. Sometimes ministers discover they are better at certain roles than others. At other times, job demands require the perfecting of certain skills. Then, too, clergy become bored with specific roles as these responsibilities become routine. Nevertheless, when one is a candidate for ministry, interest in engaging in religious activities is a definite rationale for becoming an ordained clergyperson.

One problem of ministry is that pastors try to do too many tasks, and people often expect their involvement in all of them. We will discuss the difficulties of these tendencies in chapter 4, entitled "The Hazards of Ministry." Parishioners expect ministers to fulfill the heavy role of being the "all-around person." Note, however, that there may also be an inclination toward overcommitment and overinvolvement among those who enter ministry—quite apart from parishioner expectations or actual job demands!

The guilt-proneness noted under the *feelings* section above may feed into this overinvolvement. Many ministers may feel guilty if they don't do all the tasks of ministry. They may be uncomfortable about taking time off. This tendency can lead to overwork. Surveys noted that eighty-hour work weeks are not uncommon among clergy. James Dittes suggests that ministers may suffer from "a little adult syndrome," which makes them overly conscientious and serious. He concludes, "They have difficulty playing, relaxing, compromising, and being spontaneous. It often seems as if they were born 21 years-old."[9]

A Sense of Calling

Underlying the seriousness with which clergy take their role in life may be a trait that lies somewhere between interests and feelings. This trait is "a sense of calling." From the time of Moses through the times of the disciples and the early church to the present, ministers have reported a sense of being called by God into service.

Although much Christian teaching has emphasized the "priest-hood of all believers" in which all people, including laypersons, are thought to be called by God into some type of service, a special kind of divine summons has been traditionally considered essential for those entering pastoral ministry. David, in the illustration at the beginning of this chapter, demonstrated this during summer camp when he told his friend, "I think God is calling me to become a minister."

This statement identifies David with the great majority of clergy through the ages who would affirm Jesus' statement to his disciples, "You did not choose me; I chose you and appointed you to go and bear much fruit, the kind of fruit that endures." (John 15:16, TEV) In a sense, clergy have felt they entered ministry under divine mandate. They have claimed they did not elect to enter ministry but were selected by God to be God's ministers.

We have emphasized this sense of divine calling, which has characterized ministers in the past, because it is the one feature of clergy's choice of vocation that has been most misunderstood by those outside the profession. For example, David reported that when he attempted to write a college English theme on the topic "My Call to Ministry," the professor asked him to retitle the essay "My Decision to Enter Ministry." Another example is the article entitled "Role of a Psychiatric Consultant to a Theological Seminary," in which psychiatrist C.W. Christensen expresses the opinion that those students who confessed to a dramatic call to ministry suffered from the delusions of omnipotence and deep-seated feelings of inferiority.[10]

Responding to the article mentioned above, Anton Boisen, founder of the clinical pastoral education program for ministers, wrote a letter that puts the issue into a more balanced perspective:

> There was once a time, especially in the Methodist Church, when great faith was placed in religious experiences of the dramatic, eruptive variety. Not only were conversion experiences regarded as essential to salvation, but special calls to preach were on a par with seminary training in the evaluation of a minister's qualifications. And in the history of religion in general mystical experience, the sense of being in direct communication with God, has been the ultimate source of religious authority either in personal experience or in that of some leader accepted as inspired. But Dr. Christensen's discussion of the screening of theological students leaves me with the impression that for him the old Methodist tradition has been so far reversed that a dramatic call to preach means that the candidate is so seriously ill that it is inadvisable for him ever to enter the ministry, and a sense of being in communication with God is a delusion of omnipotence induced by deep-seated feelings of inferiority.
>
> . . . I am ready to agree . . . that the tendency to accept an idea as authoritative because it seems to come from an outside source is fraught with danger. But it is important to recognize that the psychological mechanism involved is that of "inspiration." This mechanism is especially in evidence in periods of personal crisis or whenever there is intense interest or preoccupation. Under such conditions new and creative ideas do come. . . . To be sure, this creativity is achieved at the cost of judgment and perspective. . . . But I often wonder whether the patient whose eyes are suddenly opened to his unsuspected importance may not be groping after a true insight and whether his "prophetenwahn" may not have a socially valid basis.[11]

Boisen put clergy's sense of calling in a broader light than did the psychiatrist, although the psychiatrist probably spoke for many who would consider this trait a bit grandiose and messianic. While in some cases such a sense of divine mandate may feed on a weak ego, in others it may be just what it appears to be, namely, a mysterious and unique characteristic of those who would be religious professionals.

During the last twenty-five years, a concerted effort has been made to assess this sense of call in more detail. The Theological School Inventory (TSI) is the result of this effort.[12] It is widely used by seminaries to obtain a picture of the various components of students' motivation for becoming clergy.

One of the noteworthy dimensions of the TSI has been its recognition that not all people entering ministry at this time in history report a strong sense of divine call. Many candidates place more emphasis on their sense that self-evaluation of talents and interests led them to choose ministry as a vocation. Thus, the TSI measures both the sense of self-evaluation and the idea of divine summons. The two types of "leading," as the TSI terms motivation, are measured independently and a profile of the importance of each one can be obtained.

Both "natural" leading, based on introspection of one's interests and feelings, and "special" leading, based on a sense that one has been chosen by God, are dimensions of the decision to become a clergyperson. After an individual has decided on professional ministry as a vocation, has completed the required training, and has begun working in a church situation, he or she must determine how to spend the twenty-four hours available each day. We will consider these decisions in the next chapter.

Chapter 3.
What Clergy Do with Their Time

Like most weeks, this one had been hectic. In addition to his usual sermon preparation, visiting, and committee meetings, Carlos had met with the local zoning commission regarding a proposed low-income housing project. On two occasions he had also counseled with a mother whose teenage son was accused of shoplifting. Carlos looked forward to Friday afternoon and Saturday morning, when he and his family could finally go on an often-postponed camping trip.

As Carlos returned from visiting two church members in a hospital across the city, his wife, Anna, greeted him with a big hug. She then quietly reported, "Antonio called. His brother, Raphael, had a massive coronary and is not expected to live. They want you to come to the hospital this evening."

Time as Chronos and Kyros

In the theory of relativity, time is the fourth dimension that structures the three-dimensional physical world. Two or more physical objects cannot occupy exactly the same space at the same time. Time-related measures are the basic way we organize the world around us. We express these measures daily through concepts such as *age*, *temporary*, *permanent*, and *depreciation*. In and of itself, time does not change anything; rather, what happens in time affects us.

Chronological time notes the ticking off of seconds to comprise hours, days, and weeks of equal segments. Although every hour contains sixty minutes, some hours are much more significant than others. We attach meanings to time according to human experiences, giving significance to time as *kyros*, or "crisis."

These two understandings of time help to clarify some of the conflicts that ministers report in studies of ministerial satisfaction and time usage.

Some Roles Ministers Enact

For centuries, the church has divided the work of the ordained minister into components. Prophet, priest, and shepherd images have guided Christian leaders since Old Testament times. But, Mark May, in his classic study of ministry in the twentieth century, comments, "There is no agreement among denominational authorities, local officials, seminaries, professors, prominent laymen, ministers or educators as to what ministry should be."[1]

Many contemporary efforts to classify the roles or tasks of the ordained minister can be traced to the pioneering work of Samuel Blizzard in the 1950s.[2] He identified six basic roles that ministers enact and then asked them to rank the time they actually spent in each role. Using Blizzard's classifications, a recent study by Richard Blackmon showed the following results:[3]

Ranking Ministerial Roles

Role	Preferred Order	Actual Time Spent
Preacher	1	2
Pastor	2	3
Teacher	3	4
Organizer	4	6
Administrator	5	1
Priest	6	5

In this and similar subsequent studies, the most obvious discrepancy between preferred order and actual time spent is that clergy see themselves as spending much time in administrative work, which they value less than other roles. Since these are average ratings from a group, individual clergy will differ on their priorities and their definitions of roles.

Sam C. Webb, along with Blizzard, developed the Inventory of Religious Activities and Interests (IRAI) to identify ten common ministerial leadership roles.[4] The IRAI measures how much an individual likes each of 240 possible activities and interests associated with ministry. The ten roles appear in the IRAI profile in the following order:

1. *Counselor:* bringing comfort to people in need and helping people with problems
2. *Administrator:* planning, promoting, and executing various church-related programs
3. *Teacher:* teaching and directing Christian education in a local church setting
4. *Scholar:* scholarly reading, study, and research, and/or teaching in a college or seminary setting

5. *Evangelist:* various types of evangelistic outreach and contacting people for Christ

6. *Spiritual Guide:* talking about religious topics and helping people to develop their faith

7. *Preacher:* preaching and public speaking, including other types of public appearances

8. *Reformer:* seeking social justice and working for community improvement goals

9. *Priest:* liturgy, conducting public worship, and administering the sacraments

10. *Musician:* directing a local church music program (assuming training as a musician)

The other instrument that benefited from Blizzard's initial work is the Theological School Inventory (TSI), which measures interests and motivation in relation to work roles of clergy.[5] The TSI measures motivation in three ways: (1) definiteness, (2) flexibility, and (3) specific areas about which an individual is concerned.

The specific motivational areas contained in the TSI are referred to as the AIFLERP ("eye-flerp") scales. Using a forced-choice format, an individual indicates priorities by assigning a total of eighty-four points throughout seven areas of ministry:

1. *Acceptance by Others:* support of family and friends for one's decision to enter the ministry

2. *Intellectual Concern:* scholarly study and research for sermon preparation and general knowledge

3. *Self-fulfillment:* seeing the ministry as providing great personal satisfaction and sense of worth

4. *Leadership:* administrative leadership in organizing and completing tasks to reach goals

5. *Evangelistic Outreach:* personal efforts to witness to others and win them to Christ

6. *Social Reform:* personal efforts to correct injustice and deal with social problems

7. *Service to People:* pastoral care and counseling with individuals and families in need

One way to catch the flavor of these dimensions is to assume that an individual has a day with no prior commitments or plans. With these six to eight hours of unexpected freedom, how much time would he or she devote to each of the above activities or areas? In this way, a person becomes more aware of priorities for time usage as well as the expectations from others.

The Inventory of Religious Activities and Interests (IRAI) and the Theological School Inventory (TSI) are still widely used with theology students and also with people considering the ministry as a vocation. Each year approximately three thousand seminary students answer the TSI as a way of identifying their motivations and interests in the ordained ministry. The United Methodist denomination incorporates the IRAI as part of its candidacy program—the first step toward ordination. In both settings, these instruments figure prominently in programs of vocational and personal counseling concerning career and an individual's abilities, goals, and decisions in response to their understanding of God's call.

Merton P. Strommen and David S. Schuller have led a team of researchers since the mid-1970s in a large-scale study of ordained ministry. Using responses from 4,995 persons in the United States, the "Readiness for Ministry" project identified sixty-four core clusters of items that can be grouped in eleven major areas of ministry.[6]

The eleven dimensions contain nine positive and two negative clusters. These areas reflect time priorities as the way in which roles and styles are expressed in the real world. In order of importance, participants in the study rated the nine positive, general areas of ministry:

1. Open, affirming style
2. Caring for people under stress
3. Congregational leadership
4. Theologian in life and thought
5. Ministry from personal commitment of faith
6. Development of fellowship and worship
7. Denominational awareness and collegiality
8. Ministry to community and world
9. Priestly/sacramental ministry

In addition, respondents indicated that ministers should not reflect the following two negative dimensions:

10. Privatistic, legalistic style (isolated or domineering leadership styles)
11. Disqualifying personal and behavioral characteristics (undisciplined living, irresponsibility, immaturity, pursuit of personal advantage)

Strommen combined these eleven areas in four models for ministry:[7]

1. *Spiritual Emphasis.* Biblical, spiritual sensitivity, clear emphasis on being a good example, ethical living, and evangelism are emphasized.

2. *Sacramental-Liturgical Emphasis.* Sacraments and priestly concerns are emphasized.

3. *Social Action.* Openness, willingness to minister in the world, and interest in new ideas characterize this model.

4. *Combined Emphasis.* Expressions combine the above three emphases in various ways.

Time Worked per Week

Blackmon asked three hundred ministers how many hours per week they work. The distribution of results is as follows.[8]

Number of Hours Clergy Reported Working Each Week

Hours	Number	Percent
30–35	2	0.7
36–40	7	2.4
41–45	19	6.5
46–50	83	28.5
51–55	93	32.0
56 plus	87	29.9

Of this sample, 62 percent reported working at least fifty-one hours per week.

In Blackmon's study, 56 percent of the three hundred respondents reported taking one day of free time each week, 15 percent reported taking two or more days each week for free time, and 27 percent reported taking twelve hours or less of free time each week.

Time, Roles, and Job Satisfaction

In a small pilot study, Merrill Douglas and Joyce McNally asked ministers between the ages of thirty-five and sixty to chart their complete time usage for a week.[9] Respondents logged their time, using seventeen activities that were later related to six general roles of the minister. Although role categories are somewhat different from those described in the studies above, the results are instructive for ministers and their use of time.

"Lack of time" is another way to think about values and satisfactions. To say we lack time implies that activities we feel required to do crowd out other activities that we value or enjoy more. It is not the activities themselves but the valuation assigned to these activities that links time and job satisfaction.

Valuing anything is a human endeavor. To choose some activities over others leads us to the people or groups we feel will reward or condemn us for the activities and the time involved in doing them. This link between values and time usage is illustrated in the following results of a study by Douglas and McNally.[10]

Perceived Importance of Ministerial Roles and Time Allocations

Role	Value or Preferred Order	Actual Time Rank Order	Spent Hours	Actual Percent of Time
Preacher	1	2	11	20
Pastor	2	3	10	18
Theologian	3	4	8	14
Marketer	4	6	2	4
Administrator	5	1	19	34
Traveler	6	5	6	11
Total hours per week			56	

These results also confirm much of the earlier work by Blizzard and those who worked with him.

The time factor is ultimately a matter of personal relationships with others. Lists of rather clearly identifiable roles eventually express both past and present judgments and valuations of people. All roles involve choices about people in at least three ways.

First, pastors have internalized from others their expectations and assumptions about the proper balance in the work of ordained ministry. These others include teachers and mentors from the past, personal experiences, and other sources. In line with these expectations, clergy have either sought or been required to attain some level of competency in skills needed to fulfill these roles.

Second, pastors are either responding directly to the needs of other people (as in preaching, special services, visiting, and committee meetings) or they are *preparing* to respond directly to these people.

Third, clergy choose to do activities according to possible rewards and negative results they think may come from people in authority in the local church and in the denomination to which they belong.

In a study of 144 clergy, J. Conrad Glass identified twenty-five items that best expressed their satisfaction or dissatisfaction with the ordained ministry. He found that none of the items related directly to the usual role definitions of administration, preaching, priest, teaching, counseling, or visiting. Rather, eleven items expressed how clergy feel about their relationships with supervisors, congregation, family, and other ministers. Another six items focused on intrinsic aspects of one's experience in the ministry, such as being pleased with the match between personal skills and the quality of work done, and confidence before God and others that one's work is worthwhile and acceptable.[11]

These studies show that clergy do plan time for activities according to their understanding of their own skills, the resources available in their setting, and the goals they have set. Feedback that enables clergy to compare results with activities performed and time required for these tasks is a major component in producing effectiveness in ministry.

Suggestions for Time Management

Results of time management studies indicate that the following suggestions assist clergy in gaining better control of their time:

1. Log all of one's time for a full week; compare this with the study results presented in this chapter. Although one may disagree with the ways these categories are arranged, they form a useful beginning for looking at how one utilizes time.

   One helpful way to log time is to maintain an hourly activity record. Begin with the appointment schedule. Where no appointments were formally made, enter the activities that actually occurred during that hour. Create eight or ten meaningful categories around which to organize work. Color-code the week of activities according to these categories. Finally, add the entries in each category to obtain the week's tally of types of activities.

2. Quiet times can assist the minister in organizing time as well as in dealing with stress.[12] This may be meditation and devotional time followed by a brief period of planning of day's activities.

3. Identify time wasters. Among those described in the Douglass and McNally study are interruptions from phone calls and drop-in visitors; unfinished tasks that require returning to them later (with duplicate "warm up" time to get reoriented to them); routine and trivia tasks; trying to do too much in a given period; and personal disorganization, such as a cluttered desk or office.

4. Document accurate estimates of the time required to do specified tasks. Variations in the estimates will occur at times. If one sets a realistic amount of time to accomplish specified tasks, it is then easier to prioritize the tasks according to the time available.

5. Be assertive about one's own time needs. When someone requests time, the minister can decide whether or not to grant the request. One method is to state at the beginning of the contact how much time one has available. When the time is up, leave or go on to another task.

6. Plan one's work and work this plan. In addition to paper-and-pencil planners, computer programs for time management are now available. Some ministers use these programs to create a schedule for each day for weeks ahead.

7. Plan for emergencies. Although it is almost impossible to know when these will occur, statistically one can assume that sooner or later crises, unexpected meetings, and other unplanned activities will require one's time. When they do not, use the time to accomplish future planned tasks that might otherwise be crowded out by emergencies.

8. Have "next priority" tasks ready to do when someone cancels or changes an appointment.

9. Give priority to tasks that multiply effectiveness in the same amount of time. Train others to share roles of ministry. For example, some pastors invite parishioners to read selected books and articles and provide summary ideas and quotes to the pastor for use in sermons and other ways. Some administrative work can also be shared among volunteer parishioners.

10. Plan at least a day, or its equivalent, away from the church each week. Ministers frequently take less time off than they are given by their congregations. Often the minister does professional work during personal leisure time. James Dittes suggests that ministers' time use may reflect their under-lying difficulties in relaxing, playing, and being spontaneous.[13] Blackmon found no correlation between stress scores and number of hours worked but did find that stress-prone individuals do work more hours per week.[14]

11. If married, take time to be with your spouse each week. Some of this time will be in brief contacts, but at least one extended evening every week and other times together are essential to maintain a healthy marriage. Don't allow busy

days to crowd out brief hugs, kisses, and "I love you" messages that can be shared several times each day.

Insufficient time together is often reported as a problem for ministers and their spouses. In *What's Happening to Clergy Marriages?* Vera Mace and David Mace address this concern; others also have considered it in their studies.[15] In one study by Blackmon, 57 percent to 77 percent of pastors reported spending three hours or less each day with their spouse from Monday through Thursday. They reported spending three hours or more with their spouse during the remaining days of the week: Friday (61 percent), Saturday (79 percent) and Sunday (60 percent).[16]

12. Learn to work efficiently. Industry uses time-and-motion studies to help plan the flow of work for maximum use of time. Without becoming too bound by this type of analysis, clergy can consider how their office is arranged, whether it invites interruptions, how to schedule events to minimize travel time, and other ways to modify physical surroundings to maximize time usage.

Skill in word processing and other technical aids can enable a pastor to gain time. Learning to use technology is like sharpening tools before beginning work.

Time management seminars are also helpful. Roy Oswald and others at the Alban Institute and Ministers Life Resources have developed several excellent programs to assist ministers in coping with time in relation to stress and burnout in ministry.[17]

Roles, time, and expectations interact in relation to people. Clarifying and prioritizing roles and goals in relation to the needs and expectations of oneself and others are essential. Time presents clergy with the opportunity to live out their faith in daily work. This challenge should be met with wisdom and maximum effectiveness.

Chapter 4.
The Hazards
of Ministry

Note to clergy: "Warning! Ministry may be dangerous to your health!" Perhaps this warning should be stamped on every ordination parchment. These words may need to be a statement of informed consent that those who enter ministry are required to sign.

Ministry is just as much a hazardous occupation as that of highrise window washing or stunt car driving. In fact, all of the "helping professions" are hazardous in the sense that they include a high danger of burnout and a high risk of fallout. Burnout can be seen in those who become fatigued, discouraged, and overwhelmed. Fallout can be seen in those who leave one vocation and enter another. While it is not likely that clergy will plunge ten stories to their deaths, as those perched near the tops of skyscrapers might, still, they are constantly exposed to dangers that could threaten their mental health, their judgment, and their motivation.

Before considering some of these clergy hazards in more detail, think of the following two examples, which dramatically illustrate the types of issues that make for burnout or fallout in ministry.

Chris grew up in the mid-South where Southern Baptist church life heavily influenced him. He met his future wife at Sunday school; they married during their senior year at a nearby church college. Prior to going to Louisville, Kentucky, for seminary, Chris had never been any farther north than Washington, D.C. After finishing seminary, he returned south to serve as pastor in a county seat in Louisiana.

After a decade in this pastorate, Chris received a call to a mission church in Chicago. The change turned into something of a culture shock for him and his wife. Chris worked harder than ever before, and he began to feel a new sense of competence and power. Among other things, parishioners began asking him to do a significant amount of marriage counseling. Some of the wives asked to see him alone.

He felt his marriage was healthy, and he had three young daughters whom he adored. However, Chris started fantasizing that he could take the place of some of the difficult husbands whose wives he counseled. He imagined it was his duty to satisfy these women and that, if he taught them how to function sexually, this might lead to happier marriages.

One evening during a counseling session he ventured to rest his hand on the knee of one of the wives. When she did not remove it, Chris came closer to her and began kissing and caressing her. Some time later, it became known that over a two-year period Chris had been involved in sexual intimacies with over a dozen women from the church he pastored. He was asked to resign and to leave the ministry.

The case of Marshall is somewhat different. He decided on ministry as a vocation while in college. As a dramatic arts major, he intended to become an actor. However, as a result of participating in the InterVarsity group on campus, he became intrigued with the study of how scriptural principles relate to current affairs. The group influenced him so strongly that he applied for and received a Rockefeller scholarship to attend seminary after graduation.

In seminary, Marshall became interested in the pastoral ministry because it offered him the chance to preach and study. He felt this type of service would provide opportunities to invest his acting talents in a serious way. He looked forward to his first call as pastor of an independent church in a retirement community in Arizona. He thought these parishioners would have the leisure to study the Scriptures with him and to reflect on the meaning of the gospel for daily life. Furthermore, he envisioned a small community theatre for the production of serious drama. He was not disappointed. The congregation welcomed his ideas and participated enthusiastically in the variety of study and dramatic programs he presented.

He soon began to realize, however, that pastoral duties did not always allow sufficient time for studying the Bible or theology. Nor did he feel he had the leisure to prepare his sermons well, much less direct any new dramas. Many of his parishioners were either ill or in the hospital much of the time. To make matters worse, the nearest hospital was forty-five miles away. Visiting his church members in just one hospital took over three hours, and often several people in different hospitals needed his pastoral care.

After three years at this church, Marshall considered leaving the ministry. He had almost no time for doing those things he had anticipated as the fulfilling responsibilities of a pastorate. In his church, few people recovered fully from illness, and there were more sick people to visit each day. During his second year at the church, he conducted thirty-five funerals! Certainly he had never expected a pastorate to resemble this experience.

As we think of these examples, it is apparent that Chris and Marshall differed in the way the problems they encountered related to their expectations of church life. Marshall carried out his responsibilities well, but did not find them fulfilling most of the time. Chris behaved unethically but apparently enjoyed it! Furthermore, although most people would agree that Chris's justification for his behavior was erroneous, he was proactive in redefining his ministerial role to suit his interests better. On the other hand, Marshall felt trapped in the demands of his environment. It could be said that the hazard for Chris was giving in to temptation, while the hazard for Marshall was giving in to stress.

Blackmon's recent investigation of clergy problems, entitled "The Hazards of Ministry," addresses both the temptations and the stresses of ministry.[1]

Temptation Hazards

In regard to the temptation to be sexually indiscreet, Blackmon's survey of Assembly of God, Episcopal, Presbyterian, and the United Methodist clergypersons concluded that 36 percent of this group experienced feelings of sexual attraction toward members of the opposite sex in their congregation. There were no significant differences among these widely differing denominational groups. Fewer than 2 percent of all the ministers in the survey admitted that they reached the point of sexual arousal.

When asked about how much arousal they felt in different situations, over 75 percent of all the ministers surveyed reported they would be aroused occasionally or usually by those of the opposite sex who dressed seductively or were physically attractive. Of relevance to Chris's situation were the responses to the question of how often the ministers felt aroused when parishioners talked about sexual issues in counseling. Slightly over 50 percent said they occasionally experienced arousal in these situations; less than 4 percent reported they were usually aroused.

Of all the ministers in the survey, 37 percent reported they had engaged in sexual behavior inappropriate for a minister but not always with a member of their congregation. If we assume that this figure of 37 percent is representative of all clergy, studies regarding clinical psychologists and physicians suggest that ministers are much more liable to be sexually indiscreet than those two groups. Holyrod and Brodsky found that 11 percent of psychologists they surveyed had engaged in erotic contact, but less than 6 percent had participated in intercourse.[2] These percentages are similar to those reported by Kardener for physicians.[3]

What makes these comparisons even more shocking is the fact that while ethical standards for psychologists and physicians have only recently explicitly stated that sexual intimacies with clients are prohibited, the norms for clergy have included a strong implicit proscription against such behavior from time immemorial! Ministry has been a "moral" profession from its inception. The Bible includes strong affirmations of monogamy and strong disapproval of adultery.

Since the incidence of such behavior occurs three to four times more often among ministers than among other major helping professions, one can only conclude that ministry is hazardous in that the temptation to be sexually unfaithful is ever present and the resistance to this temptation is not as strong as the expectations of society or the historical standards of the profession require.

We suspect that engaging in *dual-role relationships* is what makes ministry so hazardous. Dual-role relationships are those in which people play several different roles with those they serve. While psychologists and physicians relate to those they help solely within the confines of their offices, clergy interact with parishioners in a variety of settings.

For example, Chris, with whose situation this chapter began, became indiscreet in a counseling role that, on the surface, seems similar to the setting in which psychologists and physicians work. However, unlike them, he also preached to these same women each Sunday, visited the church school classes their children attended, laughed with them at church socials, worked with them on church projects, and provided comfort in times of sickness and sorrow. He related to them in many more roles than most other helpers do. Like most ministers, Chris was inevitably involved in dual-role relationships with the women he seduced in a counseling relationship.

It is difficult to keep one's position clear while involved in a variety of relationships with others. There is a decided tendency in such situations to lose perspective, to become grandiose, and to use faulty judgment.

The core issue in dual-role relationships is the possible misuse of power. Underneath the misuse of power is a misperception of one's role. An illustration of this dynamic may be seen in a recent situation in Texas where a pastor was also a licensed counselor. An irate husband accused the pastor of sexual involvement with his wife in the course of counseling about marital difficulties the couple experienced.

Although on the surface this situation appears similar to that of Chris, described earlier, the pastor in this case denied any sexual involvement. He did admit, however, to warm feelings and frequent close contact with the couple *in his role as pastor*. He claimed that he could not avoid these types of extra-counseling relationships. He also said that he probably would have referred the couple to someone else for marital counseling had there been another trained counselor available in their small town. Furthermore, he stated that the couple trusted him and would not have entered counseling with someone else.

While the unavailability of other counselors may have been true in this case, most often it is not the case. Clergy are in danger of becoming overly influenced by their presumption of the trust that parishioners have in them and may act naively regarding their own limitations. They may be tempted to assume a messianic role they cannot fulfill. When this occurs, people are not served well, and the misuse of power for personal self-interest is clear.

The ethics committee of the church, to whom the husband in this case appealed, exonerated the pastor from the charge of sexual involvement because of lack of proof but did admonish the minister to be more scrupulous in keeping his roles distinguished.[4]

Our conviction is that while these charges of sexual intimacy may have been false, some romantic feelings and sexual indiscretions probably occurred. While society may not disapprove of sexual intimacies between consenting adults, this tolerance does not extend to those situations in which a person enters a relationship for one purpose but finds himself or herself involved in another.

The recent case involving TV evangelist Jim Bakker is a good illustration of the point. The woman with whom he became involved sexually was hired as a secretary, with Bakker as her boss. Although some may argue that she was not raped (she is an adult who participated willingly), there is no way of knowing whether she would have chosen to relate to Bakker had they met as strangers. Nor do we know what issues of self-esteem or special favors were in her mind at the time. It was not a relationship of equals. In such cases, according to most current ethical reasoning, the burden of responsibility falls squarely on the one who has the greater power.

When power is misused, "clergy malpractice" occurs, as a recent volume by H. Newton Malony, T.A. Needham, and Samuel Southard concludes.[5] Ministry cannot hide under the cloak of the separation of church and state in these matters. Clergy function within modern society, and they must live up to the ethical standards required of all other professionals who desire to help people.

Ministry is hazardous because of the ever-present temptation to become confused regarding dual-role relationships and the attendant temptation to become cloudy in one's judgment. These appear to be unique occupational hazards in parish ministry.

It may be helpful to note that sexual indiscretion are only one of a number of ways of misusing power in ministry. Preaching is another example of this possibility. Frustrations in administration or personal living can be projected onto captive audiences while filling the role of preacher. Since sermons are unique creations of individuals, they will always be vulnerable to being prostituted for ulterior purposes.

The use of sermons to project frustrations is not the only hazard in preaching. Most sermons contain personal illustrations of experiences that take place outside the church building. It is the rare minister who, at one time or another, has not violated confidentiality in telling these stories. Clergy families are the most common victims of this temptation, although many other parishioners report embarrassment because of anecdotes told about them in sermons without their permission or knowledge.

Rarely do these sermon illustrations picture the minister in a bad light. Most often, they are tales of tragedy or victory mediated by the pastor who is telling the story. The essential motivation seeps through to many listeners. There is the distinct possibility that pastors tell these stories to enhance their egos. This is obviously a misuse of power.

Although a pastor may need to struggle hard to keep sermons free from illustrations that breach confidentiality, it is always appropriate to exert such vigilance and thereby prevent preaching (another dual-role) from becoming a potential source of confounding irritations. Administration and pastoral care functions can also easily become contaminated by dual-role issues.

Earlier it was noted that ministry is hazardous because of stress as well as temptations. We now turn to a discussion of stress hazards.

Stress Hazards

Marshall, in the other situation cited earlier in this chapter, is an example of stress hazards in ministry. The demands of pastoral care in his parish were so overwhelming that he had little time to do what had attracted him to ministry in the first place. This type of *role conflict* is one of the most frequently noted stresses ministers face. It is not uncommon for clergy to burnout or fallout.

Blackmon assessed this type of hazard in the same study in which he surveyed sexual arousal and behavior.[6] In the course of conducting the study, he asked pastors to indicate whether they enjoyed performing nine common roles of ministry. He also asked them to rate the importance of each role for their jobs. Comparing "enjoyment" and "importance" gave an indication of how much stress the ministers experienced in these tasks.

The following roles were assessed: (1) serious study and writing (2) personal counseling, (3) administration, (4) discipling, (5) preaching, (6) calling/evangelism, (7) teaching, (8) leading worship, and (9) giving community leadership on crucial issues. In three of these roles (administration, discipling, and calling/evangelism), there was a noteworthy difference in the importance ascribed to the role and the enjoyment the pastors received in doing it. In each case, the ministers reported that, while they felt the role was important, they enjoyed doing it less than one might have expected. About 20 percent of the ministers reported they definitely disliked performing these roles.

Some researchers have contended that much of the stress resulting from ministers doing what they do not like is really due to disagreements between clergy and laity regarding the nature of the church and what the clergy should be doing.[7] Blackmon's study, however, did not confirm this. Over 83 percent of the ministers in his study reported agreement with their members about their job descriptions, and 82 percent felt their goals were similar to those of their parishioners.[8]

Thus, if Blackmon's findings are generalizable to all pastors, the stress experienced with job demands is not due to basic disagreements between clergy and laypersons. Stress is due to the demands of parish ministry, and these are often overwhelming. People's need for pastoral care and the organization's requirements for administration leave little time, in many cases, for pastors to engage in those tasks they find more appealing.

It is important to realize that role conflict is an occupational hazard of parish ministry. Marshall's case is the rule, not the exception. The average work week for parish ministers is over sixty-six hours. This figure is exceeded only by professions such as law and medicine.

While past research suggested that personal issues, such as family pressures and inadequate salary, were also occupational hazards in ministry, Blackmon's study did not find these concerns to be high in his research.

Other areas of potential stress for ministers include family life and retirement. Clergy family life appears to be healthy and supportive. Duane Alleman's recent study on clergy spouses confirms this impression.[9] Spouses generally feel that they have good marriages and that family life is not a problem. And although retirement benefits were some concern, present finances did not seem to pose significant concern.

We conclude, therefore, that role conflict is *the* major source of stress among ministers. Such demand overload appears to be a hazard that ministers cannot avoid. It seems as if this has been true for well over 100 years, as John Oberlin, a well-known nineteenth-century clergyperson, noted in the following statement:

> The pastor of Waldsbach [his parish], if he tries to be what he ought to be in this vast and most burdensome parish . . . is a poor dog, a beast of burden, a cart horse. He must do everything, watch everything, answer for everything. From early morning until bedtime I am occupied, hurried, crushed without being able to do half or a tenth part of what ought to be done. A decent leisure, which others can enjoy, has long been unknown to me. Who cares? Everything rests upon the pastor who meets everywhere nothing but hindrances, obstacles, delays, and red tape: and, not being able to please everybody or satisfy those who disagree with each other, must fight constantly against malevolence.[10]

The situation does not seem to have changed radically in the intervening years.

Working with the Hazards

What can be done about these hazards of temptation and of stress? In chapter 6, entitled "The Minister's Love Life," we note that the prime way of assuring against succumbing to the temptation of unfaithfulness to one's spouse is to work at keeping the marriage relationship vibrant and satisfying. Furthermore, while there is no absolute means of enabling clergy to remain free from dual-role problems, proper humility and vital avocational interests will greatly enhance the probability that ministers can function with wise judgment and keep their self-concept appropriately realistic.

In regard to the stress of role conflict, past research has suggested that clergy are peculiarly susceptible to the kind of burnout that characterizes people in the helping professions.[11] These studies suggest that 75 percent of the clergy report experiencing periods of major distress, while 33 percent of them have seriously considered leaving the ministry. At least one study, however, concluded that ministry was not as hazardous as the reports had suggested. Rayburn et al. surveyed 596 seminarians, priests, brothers, Protestant clergy, and rabbis; the sample included 288 female clergy. This study found that while clergy do experience great work overload, much role ambiguity, and excessive role responsibility, nevertheless, they experience less overall on-the-job stress and personal strain than people in other professions. Furthermore, they reported feeling they had more personal resources for dealing with stress than the general population—in spite of the fact that they experienced more interpersonal strain and had fewer recreational opportunities than most people.[12]

While there are hazards to ministry, they may not of necessity be overwhelming. The temptations and stresses of ministry to which this chapter has pointed may indeed be built-in hazards, but they need not be considered totally destructive. If the Rayburn et al. study is accepted as normative, most ministers have the resources to overcome these obstacles. The challenge is for clergy to utilize these resources.

Chapter 5.
Women in Ministry

When God created man . . .
she must have been joking.

Grace Church is looking for a new pastor. For several decades this large parish has been considered one of the best congregations in its denomination. Becoming rector of Grace Church clearly means one has achieved success. The committee on clergy/staff relations has reviewed many possible candidates and finally narrowed the choice to two persons.

Both candidates are in their mid-forties, and each has about seventeen years' experience as a senior pastor in previous congregations. The two have proven records as effective preachers, liturgists, and administrators. Parish statistics in the churches where they have served demonstrate growth in several ways. Both candidates have three children. The spouse of each candidate is a career person also and can relocate satisfactorily with their clergy mate.

Try to predict the choice of the committee. Using only the above information, one might say that it is fifty-fifty in favor of each candidate. An additional bit of information is that one candidate is a woman and the other is a man. Now try to guess the committee's choice!

Here are some opinions in the congregation:

1. "Grace Church has always been a leader. We know what a man can do. We may have too many surprises if we have a woman rector. Let's stay with the tried-and-true formula."

2. "Grace Church has grown because we took risks and developed new, innovative ministries. Having a woman as rector is merely another way of continuing to move forward in creative ministries."

3. "The gender of the rector does not matter. We want the person who can do the job best here at Grace Church."

For many reasons, opinion 2 is best supported at present by empirical studies.[1] In the longer run, opinion 3 will increasingly apply as churches move through the transition from a male-only clergy to ministerial staff whose proportions of women and men reflect the general society. Increasingly in the near future, the basic issues will likely be competence and dedication as a pastor, not whether one is male or female.

In the more distant future, will the pendulum swing to a majority of pastors being women? Seminaries in the United States report the proportion of male students under thirty years old has decreased in the last decade, while the proportion of male students over age thirty has increased. This reflects a tendency for more "second career" men, as well as women, to enter seminary in preparation for ministry. The percentage of clergywomen as pastors will continue to increase in the next decade.

Women are becoming, and will increasingly become, a normative part of the clergy picture. Total seminary enrollment in 1969 was 29,815; in 1980 the figure had jumped 66 percent for a total of 49,611. Compared with a 31 percent increase in male enrollment, female enrollment increased 223 percent and most of these were women entering degree programs leading toward ordination.[2]

In most seminaries today, 20 to 45 percent of the students are women. There are more women than men students in a few seminaries. Like their male counterparts, most of these women are preparing for parish ministry. In a majority of seminaries, the percentage increase of women and minority students has been far greater than the percentage of white men; in some instances, the white male enrollment has declined.[3]

Since for centuries only men were allowed to become ordained clergy, there has been no way of studying the extent to which privileges and problems of the clergy in all denominations were related to gender. Church leaders, both lay and professional, have tended to assume that the actions, achievements, and failures of male clergy were normative and thus that the expectations and performance of female clergy must be compared or contrasted with the male "norm."

More recently, psychological measures of vocational interests have developed scales for women as well as men. Not until 1984, however, were enough women in seminary to develop separate comparison groups for women under thirty and women age thirty and over for the Theological School Inventory.

As the increasing number of women clergy create their lifetime career records and paths, these can be compared statistically to those of men clergy. Then we will perhaps be in a better position to answer whether differences exist between men and women clergy that can accurately be attributed to the gender of clergy, rather than to other factors such as skill, experience, age, social conditions, or personality.

Two major sets of factors affect women clergy today. The first is the transition from patriarchal to egalitarian relationships between men and women in education, business, industry, and the professions, as well as in churches and among clergy. The second factor is the past individual experiences of male-female relationships that then affect how people deal with gender differences among clergy and in other situations.

From Patriarchal to Egalitarian Relationships

Regardless of whether one thinks the shift from a patriarchal, male-dominated society has gone too far or not far enough, changes have occurred. Although a majority of states have yet to pass the Equal Rights Amendment, laws and court decisions have increased equal access of women to jobs and career opportunities. Affirmative action plans continually raise consciousness regarding sexual biases in society and in the church. Women with training, competence, and experience equal to men often find that "being a woman" is a benefit to obtaining employment. While legally this cannot be acknowledged, except as part of an affirmative action plan, it is still allegedly a major factor in employment in some settings.

Transition describes the long-range movement of societies from control (whether benign, benevolent, or tyrannical) of one group by another group. Theologically, we might say the Holy Spirit continues to move us toward greater love and concern for each other in the ways we enable people to live out their vocational callings in everyday areas of work, family, and leisure.

Now that equal access of women and men to all entry-level jobs has been generally accomplished, the next few decades will likely see an increase in the percentage of women in executive levels of management. Among churches and clergy, this pattern will continue until the percentage of women clergy who pastor large parishes, serve as bishops and denominational executives, and hold other major leadership roles is in proportion to the number of women among the clergy of each denomination. Thus, in many of these settings, gender is likely to continue to be more favorable for women clergy than for men clergy with equal abilities and experience.

The concept of transition helps us evaluate the pragmatic value of the characteristics of women clergy. For example, theological schools during the 1950s and 1960s probably had significant biases against women students who intended to enter male-dominated areas of church life, such as the pastorate. Only the more determined woman would enter seminary for this purpose. Research findings indicating that women students tended to be older, to be single or divorced, and to achieve better grades may have been due, in part, to the group of women who challenged entrenched prejudices against them.

The egalitarian transition is being increasingly achieved. Students of both genders are equally welcome in most seminaries. More role models enable young women to consider ordained ministry. Whether clergy are single, married, or divorced is less a major issue. Clergy couples are somewhat more likely to be accepted by churches. Churches increasingly consider competence, commitment, energy, and related qualities of a clergyperson as being much more important than their gender.

Transition is actually one expression of a systemic approach to clergy and church life. The biological alternations between differentiation and assimilation (or integration) are also found in individual people and in the human systems we call congregations. In a sense, life is the transition between past and future. In transitions, the matrix of personal experiences of all the participants are thrust upon the larger stages of life.

Changes in Attitudes toward Women Clergy

In general, the experiences male clergy and laity have had with women clergy has favorably affected attitudes toward women pastors. Still, in one study, 65 percent of women pastors reported that their churches would prefer having a male pastor.[4] In another study, however, 45 percent of laypersons expressed a positive attitude toward women pastors.[5]

Although dramatic expressions of the increase in favor toward women clergy occasionally occur, most changes are likely to continue to happen slowly and gradually.[6] This suggests that clergy and laypersons of both sexes must continue to work toward full equality, rejoicing at dramatic changes, yet prepared to work long and hard for more subtle, but perhaps more stable, changes.

Edward C. Lehman, Jr., has suggested the following eight current factors affecting churches and women clergy:[7]

1. The current feminist movement is challenging churches to practice what they preach.

2. Church members are not monolithic in their response to clergywomen.

3. Church members are not always consistent in their response to clergywomen.

4. The predominant response of church members to women in ministry is clearly positive.

5. The resistant minority has a powerful voice in the current debates, and they influence congregational decisions far beyond the strength of their numbers.

6. Some of the differences in receptivity to clergywomen are predictable in view of other characteristics of the members.

7. Fears of congregational conflict notwithstanding, contact with women in the role of pastor tends to be a positive experience for church members. The experience transforms resistance into acceptance.

8. The denominational placement system may be the best friend of clergywomen seeking positions in ministry.

Priscilla Proctor's and William Proctor's *Women in the Pulpit* gives brief biographical sketches of female pastors.[8] Judith Wiedman's *Women Ministers* is a collection of essays by clergywomen describing their personal experience in ministry.[9] Both illustrate ways in which these factors have found expression in the lives of women clergy. Through these vignettes, one can see the variety of experiences and activities in which women clergy are engaged.

Sue Cardwell has also shown that the more successful female graduates of seminary tend to have higher intelligence, better self-image, more openness to feelings and to general human faults, alternative viewpoints, more leadership ability, and greater ability to take charge of their lives.[10] Martha Orrick noted that women clergy tend to be androgynous.[11]

Personal Experiences and Sexuality

The other major set of factors affecting women clergy are the types of experiences that they, and the people with whom they work, have had previously. The full range of experiences are found among both women and men. Some women and some men have grown up in homes in which respect was based on family members as people rather than on sex, age, or family position. This equalitarian atmosphere nurtured these people in expressing favorable attitudes toward women and men as equals before God and in society. One's gender, like one's age or other physical condition, is, at most, only one of many characteristics of a person.

In contrast, other women and other men have grown up in homes, neighborhoods, and church settings dominated by one sex or the other. This domination may have been expressed verbally in sexually linked social roles, such as "a woman's place is at home" or "men can usually do most things better than women." Or, domination may have been much more severe, such as in physical or sexual abuse that a woman or man experienced as a child or teenager.

Edwin H. Friedman describes some principles underlying these interactions. These five basic concepts from the perspective of systemic family therapy also apply to congregations. This approach can assist any clergyperson in seeing her or his professional and personal life in the context of the congregational and other systems. These are the concepts as applied to women clergy:[12]

1. *The Identified Patient.* Successes as well as problems may seem to focus upon the ordained woman as a "woman in ministry." The dynamics of the congregation (like a family) may focus upon the woman minister as the cause of whatever problems or successes the congregation encounters. Remembering that in many instances the problem or the solution is not exclusively in the woman minister as the "identified patient" helps give perspective on the underlying factors at work in a situation.

   This approach suggests that any issue that seems to be a "woman minister's issue" is actually an issue in the total system of minister, members in the church, and the congregation as a church family. The female clergyperson then is only the focal point of strains and other components in the total system.

2. *Homeostasis (Balance).* The congregation and the denomination, like a family, will try to maintain the same balance as it had in an earlier time. This is the principle of familiarity. One may not like living in hell, but at least he or she knows the names of the streets! When either the woman minister or the congregation seeks to make a change in the system, counter efforts will come from some source in order to maintain the system as it has been in the past.

   These homeostatic efforts appear in categorizing the woman minister as a sister, mother, or playmate, or in efforts to be either overly protective of the woman pastor or to make her "just one of the boys." It may show itself through comments about how the church used to be or how the church will now become because of the magical appearance of a woman minister.

If other elements in the church system change in some way coincidental with the arrival or work of a woman minister, it may be that she happens to be at the point of most pressure, rather than being the "weakest link" in the system.

3. *Differentiation of Self.* How autonomous an individual is, whether man or woman, is directly related to previous experiences of individuality and differentiation in parents, grandparents, and others in the family system. As women clergy define themselves as ministers and as people, the members of the congregation are also invited to define themselves. In a healthy system, each defines oneself and describes similarities and contrasts. In a less healthy system, one attempts to define the other person(s) in terms of previous concepts and experiences, blocking out the uniqueness of the individual.

Differentiation begins when we, as young children, are able to separate from parenting figures and yet feel confident that they will continue to love us and be available to us. This trustful flexibility in moving away and back again, of being oneself and appreciating the "selfness" of the other person also, continues to encourage identity formation and cooperation.

People who have greater difficulty getting away from parents, who are enmeshed with parents or grandparents, will possibly have more difficulty with any clergy as a new type of parental person. Every minister unknowingly elicits these types of transferences from some members in the congregation. For male ministers, these may often go unnoticed. Since most parishes have had less experience with women ministers, however, these transferences from either the woman minister or the congregation may be lifted to greater visibility. Being aware of these potentials will assist the woman minister in coping with whatever additional issues are attributed to gender factors.

4. *Extended Family Field.* This concept suggests that we continue to be heavily influenced by patterns created in past events. In simple terms, a woman whose father died at age thirty-six may fear her own husband's approaching

thirty-sixth birthday. In more complex terms, every person has at least four parents: the actual mother and father, the father that the mother told us about, and the mother that father told us about. These overlap to some extent. The pattern becomes far more complex when stepparents and/or grandparents are included in this matrix. Healthy individuals may take twenty to thirty years to completely separate themselves from their parents as parents and to become reacquainted with them as adult to adult.

The nexus between woman minister and congregation is set in the buzzing, changing force fields of the congregation as a superextended family. The church family does carry many of the same pressures and pleasures of any other extended family. These become evident as the woman minister interacts with individuals in the congregation, who then spread her influences into the lives of other members, as well as bringing to bear on her the influences of many others in and outside the congregation.

5. *Emotional Triangle.* As in geometry and geodetic domes, a triangle can be created by connecting any three points. Triangles are useful because their rigidity gives strength and reinforcement to buildings, towers, bridges, and other structures. In human relationships, triangles provide contrasts that highlight life choices.

An emotional triangle may be between three persons or between two persons and an issue or between a person, a group, and an issue. Feeling caught between two seemingly opposing groups or issues is usually a sign that one's own self is one point in the triangle.

Like her male counterparts, a woman minister may be "triangulated" in many ways in the congregation. She also brings sets of triangles from her life into these situations, forming still more emotional triangles. For example, a female parishioner with unresolved problems with her mother may triangulate the woman minister. The relationship between the woman minister and parishioner may appear to be a personal conflict when it more likely expresses this hidden dimension of the parishioner's life.

These triangles are possible interpretations of situations that women and men clergy face. All interpersonal situations involve various triangles. The triangles can be constructive and helpful when both participants are autonomous, differentiated people dealing with the realities of an important current issue in ministry. Triangles become rigid and destructive when they involve hidden or unresolved issues from the past.

Some Next Steps

With the gains already achieved, there is still need for much continuing work toward complete acceptance of women as ordained clergy. Among both women and men, and among both clergy and laity, increasingly varied patterns will likely emerge as increasing numbers and percentages of clergywomen assume more leadership roles in the churches. Some must continue to press for complete equality and acceptance. Many of both sexes would prefer to phrase this as seeking better models for ministry by both sexes, since equality with men is not in itself necessarily the ultimate goal.

It is also likely that the levels of frustration of women seeking to move into the ministry will increase, rather than decrease, in the future. "The number of women ministerial candidates is increasing at a rate much greater than the number of churches willing to accept them as ministers to their congregations."[13] This may also be the case for men in those denominations experiencing declines in finances and the number of available parishes.[14]

The inability to move to the type of pastorate one prefers reflects continuing biases against clergywomen, but it is also indicative of many other factors as well. Because of potential oversupply of pastors, many committees admitting candidates for the ordained ministry have raised their entry standards, either officially or through their decisions to delay or deny admission to persons who in earlier years they might easily have welcomed into the ordained ministry.[15] Thus, success of women clergy in the denominations will depend in part on the denominational opportunities rather than solely on gender or competence.

This suggests that church leaders of both sexes should continue to be vigilant in making admission and personnel decisions on the basis of competence and not on the basis of gender of the applicant. Among women as well as men, some will be exceptionally well qualified, many will be competent, and some will be inadequate. It is clear, however, that competent women who serve parishes can succeed as well as competent men according to any of the measures of success.

In some ways, the clergy role is unlike that of any other profession. The pastor's primary role is to enable the ministry of laypersons as the Body of Christ. This implies that the pastor's role and status are both unique and ambiguous in comparison with other professions.[16] Competence and success as a pastor is perhaps linked, not only to personal competence and commitment, but also to the nature and quality of interpersonal relations with parishioners who are more than clients, customers, patients, or other recipients of services. Evaluation efforts attempt to measure these subtle differences, yet churches and clergy must still depend heavily upon the interaction between themselves and others to enable the church to function effectively as the Body of Christ.

Some Applications

It is impossible to have exact answers for every specific situation because it is the people in the system who give rise to both issues and answers. A wide variety of specific life events calls forth a series of possible questions that can guide one in choosing how to minister. Personal decisions (such as those regarding marriage, pregnancy, parenting, and care of aging parents) can be considered when using certain questions. Professional decisions (such as whether to meet for counseling or for lunch with a male parishioner; which social issues should receive priority attention; and how to relate to women's groups in the church) also can be addressed by the following questions:

1. What is my network of support in my ministry? What are the sources of my own validation as a person and as a professional?

2. What expectations, assumptions, and satisfactions do I bring to the situation?

3. What expectations, assumptions, and satisfactions does the other person bring to the situation?

4. What cautions or preparation do I need to consider in order to work with this person?

5. If the other chooses to misinterpret my intent and actions, what independent evidence can I bring that will validate what I endeavored to do?

6. What are my goals in the situation? What will be the best possible outcome as a result of my encounter with this person?

Personal goals and expectations greatly influence a clergyperson's evaluation of specific achievements. As we note in chapter 10, "Ministerial Effectiveness," not all male clergy consider being pastor of the largest possible church as the hallmark of success. The same variations in career goals are also present among women clergy. Perhaps liberation will allow men to be as varied in their goals as women now can be. Some women, like some men, will gladly make "lateral" moves among smaller parishes. Some women will seek the top positions; others will move with their husbands. On other occasions, husbands will move when their clergywife responds to a call to a new parish and community. Clarifying one's own career goals is essential for women as well as for men. These goals also will change at different times in one's life.

Chapter 6.
The Minister's Love Life

It seemed an unlikely golf threesome. Tom had played and won often in many college and amateur golf tournaments. Chuck was still learning how to hold a golf club. Between Tom's coaching and Bill's friendly jokes about missed shots, the threesome had made it to the fourteenth hole.

Married nearly eighteen years, Tom and his wife, Becky, have three healthy, happy children. Tom is now in his fourth year as rector of the Church of the Good Shepherd. Chuck is single and the pastor of St. Barnabas Church in a nearby suburb. Bill, a friend of Tom's since college, is a successful salesman for a medical supply company.

When Chuck missed an easy putt, Bill commented, "That's just the way my third marriage ended. Every time I tried to do something nice for Jan, she said if I really cared for her, I would stay home more often. I couldn't do that. There's too much going on out in the world."

As they walked to the next tee, Bill continued, "Tom, you've really missed a lot in life. You and Becky met in college, and you've never really known another woman well. After three marriages and several other relationships, I know how to handle women, give them a good time, and leave before it gets sticky."

"Well," replied Tom, "You have been with more different women than I have, but you haven't really known them like Becky and I know each other. Together we have struggled to make our wants and needs fit our income, to serve the parish and yet have family time, and to encourage our kids in their growing years. Through both joys and disappointments, we have kept our romance alive across the years. We know each other better today, yet there are still areas in which we need to grow in our love for each other."

"I guess I'm different from you both," Chuck mused. "The parish requires so much time that marriage is not an option for me right now. The one woman I might have married did not want to marry a minister. Occasionally, I may take a female friend to a social gathering, but I have no plans for marriage."

Is the Minister's Love Life Different?

We can answer this question with both no and yes.

In one sense, the minister's love life is the same as for people in other walks of life. They meet someone, develop a loving relationship, and make a commitment to marriage. In Christian traditions that allow ordained clergy to marry, the marriage rate is typically as high as that of the general population. Thus, over 93 percent of ministers will marry at least once. And like others, some clergy will never marry.

Some married ministers will divorce, and most of these will remarry. The percentages of ministers who divorce has increased in the last twenty years, perhaps due in large part to the increasing tolerance and acceptance of divorced ministers by local churches and denominations. Whether the rate will eventually reach the 40-50 percent divorce rate in the general population depends on the church's understandings of marriage as well as on the increasing acceptance of divorce for clergy.

In several ways, the love life of ministers is different from the general population and from other professions such as medicine, law, politics, and business.

First, in becoming ordained, an individual vows to serve God through the church and to place this commitment above all other human commitments. This vow excludes any and all other commitments as being equal, although other commitments certainly can come in lower priority in relation to the ordination vow. The minister's call is considered to be from God and thus to transcend any other commitment the ordained clergy may make.

No other career group commonly claims divine authority for entry or continuation in its line of work. Many other professional and business groups, however, do pressure their members to place work first. The work ethic of the Western world, not just a Protestant work ethic, has tended to assume that an individual must give first priority to work. To be truly professional in medicine, for example, means that the physician vows to place the life and health of his or her patients above personal and family life. Many corporations expect their employees, especially those who want to advance in the company, to give first allegiance to the company, rather than to their families or other priorities.

Second, until recent times the church usually assumed the minister's spouse and family would fit into the congregation and its community without questioning, complaining, or disturbing. In some denominations with a centralized governmental structure, the traditional appointment process assumes the church has authority to place its ministers wherever the denominational leaders consider best. Appointments are intended to maximize the fit between the needs of a congregation and the talents and abilities of a particular minister. So long as the minister's spouse does not question this appointment, the system works well for those in authority and usually for most ministers.

Today, with over 60 percent of clergy wives holding full-time jobs or involved in careers, and probably with nearly all clergy husbands being in paid work, centralized appointment structures have been increasingly modified to include consideration of the needs of the minister's spouse.

In denominations with a congregational form of governance, each congregation calls its ministers in order to maximize the effectiveness of a local church in ways the leaders consider most appropriate. The additional variations in church government still focus on the minister as one who will give service to others without restraint.

Third, the spouse and family of the minister are more directly involved in his or her work because they usually attend the same local church the minister serves. There is typically much more overlap between the minister's professional role and the personal network of friendships in a congregation than is true for other professional groups. For example, difficulties between the clergy and church members may directly affect the minister's spouse and family, who may have friendships with the families of these members. Again, today there are more possible models; therefore, the options for ministers and their families are becoming more like the options of families of other professional and business groups.

Through the centuries, Christian groups have dealt with this fundamental conflict in commitment priorities in various ways. In some periods and among some groups, ordained clergy have been prohibited from marriage because church authorities thought married life detracted from one's allegiance, time, and energy available for ministerial work. During some periods of history, sexual intercourse was linked to sin. At other times, the slower travel and communication—which missionary outreach on the frontiers entailed—made commitment in marriage very difficult.

Fourth, the time schedule of clergy is often "out of sync" with the rest of a community. Clergy must make contacts when families are available, which is typically evenings and weekends when their own families most want the minister at home. Pastors must work on Sunday. As in other professions, clergy are subject to emergency calls at any hour and may be called into crisis situations at any time.

Of course, many people in other lines of work also have work schedules that seem out of sync with the community. Consider many who work in restaurants and entertainment areas and must serve those who spend their leisure time using these services. Workers in other professions are also subject to emergency and/or overtime work requirements.

Ministers possibly have as much total time with their spouses and families as most other workers. In Duane Alleman's study, between 70 and 80 percent of the wives reported having at least two or more hours each day with their pastor husbands, excluding meals and sleep.[1] If one considers a worker with a fixed schedule of an eight-hour-per-day job and with one to two hours in commuting time, then having two to three hours together after dinner in the evening would be quite typical.

While pastors' schedules are often different and perhaps at times more hectic than other workers, they have greater control of their schedules most of the time than people employed in other occupations. For example, ministers whose children are not in school can arrange to have free times with their families during the week when most people are at work.

These four dimensions—one's sense of calling; the dual-career (or dual-job) couple; the family's direct involvement with the minister's work; and atypical time schedules—form the context in which the minister's love life is set. Let us now consider marriage as the central love life in which the majority of ministers are involved.

Models of Marriage

Just as there are variations in the minister's understanding of the calling and profession of ordained ministry, so there are variations in the models and visions of marriage. William J. Everett has described four major Christian views of marriage:[2]

1. *Sacrament.* The couple participates in symbolic ways in the paschal mystery, the little school, and the household of faith aspects of the Christian community, living these out in their marriage.
2. *Vocation.* Marriage is the response of the spouses to God's

call to marriage. Spouses may pursue specific goals or may see themselves as occupying a special status as married people.

3. *Covenant.* The will and intent of the partners is to be unconditionally with and for each other, as God has covenanted with Israel and us, and in which the marriage in some way becomes an analogue of the divine-human encounter.

4. *Communion.* The emphasis is on God's grace operating through human nature, becoming a pilgrimage of personal growth that also reaches out to influence others.

Depending on whether one emphasizes the individual, the couple, the family, or the larger household (extended family and/or friends), each of these basic views of marriage takes on additional special meanings.

Conflicted Clergy

Two fundamental vows come into conflict for clergy who marry. We have seen many variations on the nature of the ordination vow and on the nature of the wedding vow. Nevertheless, at some level the ordained minister will encounter a fundamental conflict between these two vows.

Clergy who marry make an exclusive vow to their spouse. To "forsake all others" implies not only sexual exclusiveness but also the exclusion of any commitment that ranks before the commitment to one's spouse. Commitments to parents, children, extended family members, friends, and any others must rank behind the fundamental commitment to one's spouse. From the marriage vow perspective, commitments to one's vocation are likewise to be placed after the vow to one's spouse. This sets up a major conflict for married clergy.

Other groups have lifted up the values of Christian marriage for their ordained clergy. The more settled times of the late nineteenth and early twentieth centuries in the United States gave rise to the traditional assumption that a minister would be married when called to a church. In those instances when he (women had not yet been accepted for ordination) was not married, most parishes could find families with an eligible, desirable daughter who would make an excellent wife for the single parson. In spite of unofficial social encouragement to marry, however, no denomination has officially required its clergy to be married as a condition for ordination.

Love and Sexuality

Perhaps the typical interpretation of "love life" emphasizes the romantic-sexual-pairing relationships that adults form. With this as our focus, let us place adult sexual relationships in the context of the full range of love.

The fundamental dimension of marriage is love with its many synonyms; care, nurture, acceptance, concern, warmth, presence, genuineness, vulnerability, unconditionality, maintenance. This is the goal, the end, the purpose of marriage, although we may also note its presence in many other human relationships.

The second dimension of marriage is power, the means to achieve the end of love. Its synonyms include resources, action, control, planning, task orientation. Power is the ability to achieve the end of love for oneself and for the other under the faith relationship with God.

The minister's love life is both a system and part of larger systems. In these systems are people, resources, and time.

Along the *person* dimension are the following:

1. Love for parents, siblings, grandparents, and other members of one's family of origin
2. Love for one's spouse and children as one's family of pro-creation
3. Love for one's friends, in-laws, neighbors, and work associates
4. Love for one's community, country, and world
5. Love for God as known in Jesus Christ and the Church as the community of believers in Christ

Along the *resource* dimension are these elements:

1. Money as the ability to acquire and exchange goods
2. Skills for work, play, leisure, and recreation
3. Interests and activities
4. Sexual activities and expressions
5. Housing as protection from the elements and facilities to enable activities
6. Safety from physical, sexual, and other abuses
7. Communication of inner perspectives and decisions into the external world of people

Along the *time* dimension are the following elements:

1. Past, present, and future in the context of one's understanding of historical sequences

2. Cause and effect
3. Parallel events
4. Systems of relationships
5. The progression of time (chronos)
6. The meanings of time (kairos)

Through time, God asks us to act as real people who influence other real people and events.

Family of Origin as Context for Sexual Decisions

One's family of origin is a group of people of various ages and both sexes into which we are both born and adopted. Through birth, we made our physical appearance in the world. The people involved in that birth, such as a mother, father, and other relatives, decide to keep (adopt) or reject the new baby. So far as we know, we did not initially choose these parents and relatives, yet they exert major influences on us. These experiences become the first standard against which we measure other experiences.

Some people grow to adulthood supported and nurtured by constant, unconditional, wise, and caring love from a consistent network of family and friends. At the other extreme, some people are thwarted and dwarfed by family experiences that hurt, reject, stifle, and wound, so that, by comparison, being psychotic or drug dependent or bitterly aggressive or withdrawn are more pleasant and desirable than the continuing hurts they experienced in childhood and adolescence.

As a result of these experiences in childhood and adolescence, adults bring needs, wants, and expectations to their encounters with other adults of each sex. These family-of-origin experiences greatly influence the meaning individuals seek from their role and work as clergy in the church, as well as how they act with a love partner, whether spouse or "significant other." To call God "Father" or "Mother" involves feelings of "good father" and "good mother" and/or "bad father" and "bad mother" that one experienced earlier in life. To the extent that a person received love from parents and other care-givers (siblings, other relatives, child-care people, neighbors, teacher, and others), he or she is freed and enabled to both give and receive love in adult relationships such as marriage.

Those who are familiar to us, our family, constitute a system into which we fit ourselves in order to establish our own uniqueness and maximize our acceptance, affirmation, affection, and identity as people. To be able to see how this drama unfolded is difficult yet absolutely necessary. It is part of our launching from our family of origin, part of our "divorcing" those people and that power structure, in order to accept those people as adults before God. The Creator does not intend that we continue as children forever but rather that we become free, autonomous people who are so inner-directed by God's love and Spirit that we act to bring peace, safety, and care to others.

To the extent that experiences in our family of origin crippled us by preventing us from developing into energetic, caring adults, we may then distort some combination of roles in an effort to compensate for past lacks and losses. In the case of clergy, this may be exemplified in the conflict between the ministerial role and spouse/family roles. Efforts at compensating are doomed to failure, however, because they focus on the past rather than the present. These efforts may show up in being aloof from spouse and family, putting down one's spouse, trying to prevent a spouse from being involved in the pastor's work, or being afraid to make decisions that one's spouse may not like.

There is not room in this chapter to present details of how these contexts of ordination vow and marriage vow perspectives have an impact on each marital and sexual situation. We can suggest some major highlights that can be followed up in additional ways.

Successfully Married Ministers

"I haven't had a full evening at home in the past six weeks."

"Sex would be more fun if you would remove your beeper."

The majority of marriages among ministers are successful, according to a study by Richard Blackmon.[3] With all the talk about difficulties, divorce, and other disasters in marriages of clergy, it is easy to overlook the other side of the picture. Typically, successful marriages do not receive publicity. Little in them produces gossip.

Marriages of clergypersons (with one or both spouses as ordained ministers) share these qualities with other successfully married couples. In a successful marriage, each partner exhibits the following characteristics:

1. Is relatively free from his or her own family of origin and from the family of origin of the partner
2. Has clear, realistic expectations for self and for partner
3. Is able to express care and affection appropriately to the spouse
4. Shares with the spouse common goals and life-styles
5. Is able to cooperate, to confront difficulties and disagreements, and to resolve conflicts

6. Is autonomous and has some individual times and activities apart from the spouse
7. Is committed to growth through staying in the relationship
8. Can voice feelings and be vulnerable
9. Can respect the boundaries between self and other
10. Enjoys humor, spontaneity, surprises, and celebrates togetherness
11. Accepts the unfinished nature of the couple's relationship as part of their continued growth; views events in the relationship as "better or worse" rather than "absolutely perfect or impossible"
12. Acknowledges the good intentions of the other and assists the partner in communicating these more effectively
13. Has developed financial plans and procedures with the spouse that satisfy themselves and their creditors
14. Has a long-term healthy vision of their marriage so that difficulties can be placed in the context of the overall success of their relationship
15. Could succeed in life alone (has options), but consciously chooses to be with the partner

In addition, successful clergy marriages cope with these issues in ways that satisfy both spouses and the congregations they serve. These marriages exhibit the following characteristics:

1. Manage time schedules well, whether daily, weekly, monthly, or yearly
2. Accept the reality that they will probably move to another congregation sooner or later
3. Have ways to clarify couple vs. congregation expectations in constructive ways and to negotiate conflict between these expectations
4. Maintain friendships beyond the church they serve, in addition to friendships they may develop among members of the current church
5. Seek counsel and consultation when they encounter difficulties they cannot seem to handle alone
6. Cope with strains constructively so that they do not become major causes of stress on the marriage

Troubled Marriages

"You run the church, and I'll run the home."

"You don't love me like you used to."

Troubled marriages among clergy typically are missing one or more of the elements just cited about successful marriages. Little troubles, if unattended, can become big troubles.

The common visible areas of distressed marriages usually appear as difficulties in money matters, sexual activities, drug abuse (alcohol and other drugs), and/or violence (verbal, physical, and/or sexual). These and other expressions are actually symptomatic of more fundamental trouble in the marriage. The following are typical problem sources:

1. Inability to disengage from past relationships or hurts, usually in one's family of origin

2. Lack of skill for expressing warmth, caring, and concern to partner

3. Interactive patterns that maintain harmful behaviors

Divorce

"I can't believe that our pastor is getting a divorce. If ministers don't stay married, then who can?"

"I guess God didn't join us after all."

Divorce is the culmination of a long series of hurts and sadness for each partner. Just as it takes two to marry, it also takes two to divorce. Among many aspects, divorce means the following:

1. You are no longer married, yet you must continue to deal with each other, either regarding children or money or perhaps in coping with memories from the period when you were married.

2. Some people will understand, but many will not.

3. The minister may be asked to leave the church.

4. The nonminister spouse will usually have greater adjustments, such as moving from the parsonage or losing friends in the congregation, if the minister stays as pastor or staff member in the church.

Second Marriages

When the ordained minister remarries, both spouses have adjustments in addition to those facing nonclergy couples. These include adjustments to a new or different residence; "his," "hers," and perhaps "our" children; financial obligations to previous spouse and/or children; and structuring the larger networks of kinship and friends.

In a study of women in remarriage to clergy, Douglas Miller found that nonclergy wives were more aware of stresses than were their clergy husbands.[4] Step-parenting and disciplining of children were major concerns. These women typically had high ego strength, strong self-esteem, deep individual self-worth, and a strong desire to lessen the stress.

Successful remarriages (second marriages) are created from the same set of elements as a successful first marriage. In addition, important feelings about any previous spouses must be resolved, reviews of personal skills that need to be developed must be made, and adjustments among role expectations and assumptions in relation to the ministry need to be accomplished.

Homosexuality among Ministers

Blackmon found that slightly less than 10 percent of the three hundred ministers in his study reported that they were sexually attracted to members of their own sex.[5] Attraction does not imply active homosexual contacts, although some therapists suggest this rate is higher than churches want to admit. In the few Christian traditions accepting homosexuality as a legitimate life-style, the percentage of homosexual ministers would, of course, be higher. This rate is influenced by homosexual ministers coming to these denominational groups because they are rejected by others.

Theological orientation is related to the rates of homosexual attraction and extramarital affairs among ministers. The reported rates are lower for more theologically conservative ministers. This may be the effect of the type of theology itself or may indirectly reflect other factors. Among these are stricter rules about one's conduct, greater obedience to authority and rules, and fewer opportunities for these behaviors. Differences in the marriage and family expectations and satisfactions of ministers are also very significant in these areas.

Extramarital Affairs

"The mistress in my husband's life is the entire church. How can I compete with God for my husband's attention?"

"I knew something was going on when I realized the pastor and the church secretary were all alone every week at the church."

"My husband never wants me to go with him to the regional pastors' meetings, and he always stays longer than most other ministers whom I know."

Extramarital affairs usually express personal needs and desires that are not being met in the marriage. Janelle Warner and John

Carter found that pastors and their spouses are more lonely and have lower marital adjustment than comparable nonclergy couples.[6] Since so many deep meanings are attached to sexual behaviors, extramarital affairs involving ministers bring additional complications beyond those of other couples.

1. The minister is trusted to be alone with anyone and not take advantage of the professional relationship. A sexual affair breaks this trust and often causes other people of both sexes to be much more cautious and distrustful of the minister.

2. Since most, if not all, congregations are strongly opposed to extramarital sexual relationships, public knowledge of a minister's affair will almost certainly bring some type of public disciplinary action. Often this means probation, temporary suspension from ministerial duties, or termination of one's license as a minister.

In Blackmon's study of three hundred ministers (fourteen of whom were women), he found that, depending on denominational affiliation, between 20 and 47 percent of them reported having had physical contact with a church member other than their spouse.[7] Since physical contact is a broad term, Blackmon also asked if the minister had ever had sexual intercourse with anyone other than his or her spouse. The percentage was almost the same. Between 18 and 45 percent answered yes to this question. Then, in answer to the question of whether this other person was a member of the minister's congregation, between 3 and 20 percent answered affirmatively. (The span in percentages refers to different denominations—37% was the average.)

In interpreting his study, Blackmon suggests that the incidence of sexual intercourse between ministers and nonspouse members of the congregation is probably higher than these reported percentages. This incidence is three to eight times higher than the rate of sexual contacts between clinical psychologists and their patients, and higher than the rate for physicians and their patients. By comparison, the estimated rate of extramarital sexual affairs among the general population is approximately 45 to 55 percent, a rate that is affected by many factors in different segments of the population.[8]

Extramarital sexual contacts between ministers and members of their congregation occur more often than we want to admit. They are a major concern for many ministers and for the church in general. The following are some ways of coping effectively with this concern:

1. Raise awareness among ministers about the serious consequences to the church and to the minister for any clergyperson to have inappropriate contacts with others, especially church members who must be able to trust their pastor(s) without any question.

2. Place inappropriate sexual contacts by ministers in the context of larger marriage, family, congregational, and professional dynamics that involve individual self-esteem, affectional needs, and love.

3. Provide specialized, and absolutely confidential, professional assistance to ministers, spouses, and other people involved with a minister in any type of sexual affair.

4. Increase the availability of marriage enrichment retreats and other positive marriage support networks for ministers and their spouses.

Single Ministers

"Ministers are so holy that they would never think of sex."

"Preachers have more hands than anyone I've ever dated."

"There is a certain very eligible bachelor who would be a great husband for you. I know women clergy may find it difficult to find the right husband."

There are at least three types of single clergy: those who have never married but plan to do so later; those who were formerly married; and those who have consciously decided never to marry.

The following comments are primarily for individuals who have decided never to marry:

1. Express singleness as a life-style equally as viable as marriage, without defensively criticizing marriage or singleness.

2. Clarify how you will live out your own sexuality in the context of expectations that single people are always celibate and of suspicions that single people have secret sexual relationships with one or more partners.

Each of these maritally related statuses is a temporary or permanent life-style. To be successful, a clergyperson must clarify his or her sense of vocation and the vow taken as an ordained person, and his or her understanding of the marital promise and life as a couple. Although reading books can help, much more important is expressing love to one's spouse, if married, and to one's relatives, friends, and associates. Now is the time to act.

Chapter 7.
Spouse and Parish

Every hour it took to drive to the camp was well worth it. A gentle breeze quietly echoed through tall evergreens rising majestically beside lazy gurgles of water in a nearby stream. Cool, clean air surrounded everyone. What a beautiful setting for this first-ever ecumenical retreat for pastors and their spouses.

Four women paused to read the memorial marker on the northeast corner of a nicely furnished cabin: "Erected in memory of Mrs. William Johnson, a faithful pastor's wife and mother to her children. The Women's Guild of St. Mark's Church, 1953."

Their conversation revealed some of what they thought about the plaque:

"I wonder what she would say to us today?" Sue questioned.

"We don't even know her first name," answered Betty. "What woman today wants to be known only as 'Mrs.'?"

"She must have done something very special, which her local church appreciated, for them to build this comfortable cabin in her honor," Cathy continued. "No one will ever do that for me."

A bit surprised, Sue responded, "What do you mean?"

"I'm just not willing to play the piano, teach Sunday school, lead the women's society, and be a servant to my husband and his congregation." Cathy retorted, a bit angry. "I want to be an individual, just like any other wife in the community. If people in the church like me, fine; if not, then that's their problem."

"And your husband's problem as their pastor," added Sue. "I really like being a teamworker with Jack. I feel just as called to being a minister's wife as he feels called to the ministry."

A sudden silence amplified the rustle of leaves. Jan traced the jagged mortar lines in the flagstone wall. "I started not to come," she began. "I'm now an ordained minister, and I serve as a co-pastor with my husband, Bill. So I'm a pastor as well as a pastor's wife. Sometimes I'm not sure which role I am in. If we are both pastors, neither of us has a spouse in the traditional sense. Sometimes I think it would be nice to have a 'wife' to do all those details I don't have time to do as a pastor."

Unnoticed, Jim had stepped over to see what was so interesting about the cabin. Seeing the plaque, he mumbled, "I'm not sure I belong here. My wife is a pastor, and I'm the only pastor's husband at this meeting. I want to support Barbara in her work as pastor, but at times neither of us quite knows how to do it."

Multiple Models

There are several models for the relation between a pastor's spouse and the parish. It is easy to assume that in some bygone day there existed a unitary, clear model called the "traditional clergy wife." But then—as now—there were varieties of models. Some pastors' wives did "play the piano, teach Sunday school, and lead the women's society." But some of those wives had careers as school teachers or nurses or otherwise worked outside the home. Some were not musically talented; others had little involvement in the affairs of their pastor-husband's parish.

Contrary to some views, the involvement of the pastor's wife in the parish of her husband has changed little in the past twenty years. A comparison of the research by William Douglas in 1965 with the research of Duane Alleman in 1987 shows these percentages:

Percentage of Pastors' Wives Involved in Husband's Ministry

	Douglas (1965)[1]	Alleman (1987)[2]
Very involved, a teamworker	21	29
Very involved in a background, supportive way	64	53
Involved, but no more than if he were in another vocation	15	15
Not interested, rather antagonistic	0	3

In his study of ministers' wives in the Presbyterian, United Methodist, Assembly of God, and Episcopal denominations, Alleman also identified five general models for involvement of pastors' wives in their husbands' ministry. Of the 226 wives who categorized themselves in one of these models, 54 percent considered themselves to be a "background supporter"; 21 percent a "teamworker"; 5 percent a "co-pastor"; 13 percent an "individual"; 2 percent "disinterested"; and 4 percent "other."

Of the respondents, 60 percent answered that they would not change their type of role involvement. Of the remaining 40 percent, 12 percent of the total sample would prefer to be an "individual with no more responsibilities than any other church member"; 11 percent would choose to be a "background supporter"; 10 percent, a "teamworker"; 2 percent, a "co-pastor"; and 2 percent, "uninvolved."[3]

As we consider how each of these models can be implemented in a parish, we will also attend to implications of the family systems approach for these solutions. In addition, it is important to remember that in each of these models some wives work outside the home, but others do not. There is some indication that preferring a specific model is related to the individual's theological position, ages of children, level of education, and the size of the church served by the pastor-husband.

Models of Clergy Spouse Involvement with Parish

These models are arranged in order from the spouse being least involved to *most* involved in the parish.

Disinterested Model

The "disinterested" spouses comprised only 2 percent of the 226 respondents in the Alleman study. Another 4 percent indicated a model other than the ones listed below. Very few spouses reported being disinterested or antagonistic to the work of the church. Nearly all spouses would not try to get their spouse-pastor to leave the ministry. Compare this with Richard Blackmon's study.[4]

Apparently it is rare for a pastor's spouse to consciously and intentionally try to cause trouble for her husband-pastor. Where the spouse is not interested in the church, she will more likely either not attend, rarely attend, or perhaps attend a different congregation.

One extreme example of disinterest occurred when the wife of the pastor of a small church persisted in mowing the lawn of the parsonage, which was situated next door to the church. This would probably have been acceptable except for the fact that, dressed in shorts, she operated the power mower during the time of the morning worship service, easily visible (and audible) through the clear glass windows of the sanctuary!

It is likely that a spouse's deliberate show of disinterest is as much a reflection of her or his current relationship to the spouse-pastor as it is a theological statement about the church or life.

Individual Model

The individual model was preferred by 24 percent of United

Methodist wives, 19 percent of Presbyterian wives, 10 percent of
Episcopal wives, but none of the Assembly of God wives. This
model was more likely to be held by wives in the largest churches,
wives whose children were of college age or older, wives with
liberal theological views, and those with graduate education
degrees.

The individual model takes as its guide the freedom to participate or not in the same way that any other layperson may choose
whether to be involved in the life of the local congregation. The
typical spouse who prefers the individual model probably has
these characteristics:

1. Advanced education or training
2. More options for church involvement
3. Distinguishes marriage roles from church roles
4. Engagement in a career, hobbies, or other interests

It is important to distinguish the individual model from the disinterested model in this study. In the individual model, the spouse
affirms the Christian faith and the church, yet expresses her faith
in actions that are separate from the local parish. By contrast, the
disinterested spouse may feel hurt or angry and may oppose the
spouse-pastor in overt or covert ways. Going their independent
ways does not necessarily mean that spouses are dissatisfied with
each other or with the church.

Background Supporter Model

Approximately 50 percent of all the ministers' wives (and 76
percent of the Episcopal wives) in the sample obtained by Alleman
were satisfied being a background supporter to their pastor-
husband. This role is probably more compatible with a larger
church where a capable staff of leaders, in addition to the pastor's
spouse, is available to share ministerial responsibilities.

Women who have additional personal interests outside the
church are likely to choose the background supporter role. They
tend to have some college education and have children who are in
junior and senior high school.

What constitutes a background supporter will differ among
couples. Background support can come in one or more of the
following ways:

1. Regular participation in the life of the congregation, such as
   attendance at worship, participation in church school, and
   attendance at some of the general congregational functions
2. Willingness to attend and participate with one's pastor-

spouse in activities designed for ministers and spouses. These may be social and/or continuing education events sponsored by local groups of churches, ecumenical agencies, or denominational offices.

3. Interest in hearing the pastor-spouse discuss events of his or her work, exploring possibilities, and consulting together on plans and solutions for parish concerns

4. Creation and maintenance of a pleasant home atmosphere

5. Adjustment without extensive complaints to the unexpected emergencies and shifts in family schedules due to parish needs

6. Prayer, worship, Bible reading, and other devotional experiences together as a couple

7. Avoidance of activities that would create difficulties for the pastor-spouse

Teamworker Model

Women who preferred the teamworker model tended to have a more conservative theology, a high school education, and to be in smaller churches.

Teamworker spouses may do many of the things that background supporters do. In addition, teamworker spouses may show other traits:

1. Take a more active leadership role in the church as a church school teacher, leader in women's work, musical leader or accompanist

2. Go with their pastor-spouse on visits to homes, hospitals, and other contacts with parishioners

3. Actively participate in evangelistic outreach and in contacting prospective members of the church

4. Attend business meetings of the church with their pastor-spouse

Co-pastor Model

It is not as clear how the co-pastor model may differ from the teamworker model. Some co-pastor spouses may also be ordained clergy, and these situations will be considered in chapter 8, "Dual-Careers in Clergy Life." Some spouses may perceive themselves as a co-pastor although the church sees them more as a teamworker or background supporter.

Of the twelve wives in the Alleman study who identified themselves as "co-pastors," five were in the Presbyterian and United Methodist denominations, which ordain women on the basis of master of divinity or other graduate degrees, and seven were in the Assembly of God denomination, where ordination does not always require advanced education.

Motivations for Ministry and Parish Involvement

Some ministers' wives feel they also are called by God to the work of being a minister's wife. Perhaps some single male ministers have been confronted by a woman who announced that she was called to be his wife! Many ministers welcome this sense of dedication and commitment from their wives.

Among the four denominations in the study, 66 percent of Assembly of God wives, 53 percent of Presbyterian wives, 38 percent of United Methodist wives, and 33 percent of Episcopal wives reported they felt called to be "a minister's wife or to full-time Christian ministry." By contrast, 17 percent of Assembly of God, 34 percent of Presbyterian, 49 percent of United Methodist, and 47 percent of Episcopal clergy wives reported that they were "not called" in this way. The remainder reported they were not sure about this type of calling.[5]

Overall, the motivations of ministers' wives to participate in their husbands' ministry and parish are substantially the same as twenty years ago.

Motivations of Pastors' Wives for Parish Participation
(by Percentage)

Motivation	Douglas (1965)[6]	Alleman (1987)[7]
Call to be minister's wife or to full-time ministry	27	30
Belief in the purposes of the church	33	34
Desire to contribute through useful work	27	21
Desire to be close to husband *	13	12
Because it is expected of me *		3

(* combined in Douglas study)

This suggests that regardless of the model for parish involvement, spouses see themselves as having positive motivations.

There are several possible obstacles to women being able to actualize their preferred type of involvement with their pastor-husbands and the parish. The Alleman study found the following percentages:[8]

Obstacles to Wives' Preferred Involvement with Pastor-Husbands

Obstacle	Percent Yes	Percent No
Congregational expectations	43	57
Self-expectations	41	59
Husband's expectations	39	61
Family responsibilities	37	63
Job responsibilities	34	66
Lack of training	20	80
Other	22	78

About 65 percent of the wives in this study experienced a convergence between their desired and their actual involvement in the parish.[9]

Some Suggestions and Applications

Each of these models involves the triangle between minister, spouse, and congregation.[10] Triangles can be valuable as support if they involve three different points of view that mutually communicate, support, and enhance one another. They can be destructive when any pair of the three isolate and shut out the third viewpoint.

Several guidelines can help spouse and pastor as the spouse and parish relate:

1. Pastor and spouse, as husband and wife (spouses of women ministers are considered in the next section), must agree on the general model they want. If not in complete agreement, they must at least agree to disagree in supportive, friendly ways.

2. Both spouses must take personal responsibility for the choices they make without blaming the congregation or its committees for their situation.

3. The church parish, through its pastoral relations committee or other appropriate unit, also needs to clarify the expectations they want in their pastor's spouse.

4. Depending on the tradition of the church and the models of the pastor and spouse, the pastoral relations committee and the pastor and spouse can periodically discuss together their common ministries. This may be done in an official meeting, but in most instances it is probably accomplished in informal settings involving the pastor, spouse, and key church leaders.

Most spouses would probably prefer not to meet in an official capacity with a church committee, since they believe that the church "hires" their spouse-minister, not the nonminister spouse. Some spouses, most likely those who select the independent model, will probably refuse to enter into any official discussion with such a committee, since they consider the church committee or representatives to have no authority over the spouse. Many more spouses would probably prefer to talk with their spouse-pastor, who then can discuss any matters with the appropriate committee.

The key to this fourth suggested step is to eliminate the potential for secret administrative expectations concerning the spouse and to create an open atmosphere among all involved. This can avoid clashes between assumptions by the couple and assumptions of the congregation.

5. Clergy spouses need to evaluate their talents, skills, and interests in order to find areas of service they enjoy both inside and outside the church. This minimizes unnecessary competition.

6. Conflicts between spouse and parish probably express unresolved past issues in either the spouse, the pastor-spouse, or people in the church. Thus, the solution to the apparent issue may actually be at a quite different point.

7. All involved can assume that pastor, spouse, and parishioners intend to serve the Lord. Until clearly proven otherwise, assume that all participants mean well for each other.

When the Pastor Is a Woman

Few studies of husbands of women ministers have been made because the ordination of women is a very recent phenomenon. A study of fifteen women clergy, ages 30 to 60, by L. Guy Mehl showed that the husbands of these clergywomen were middle-class professionals.[11] Women clergy may find conflicts between traditional sex roles and institutionally based clergy roles but not between clergy and family roles.[12]

Exact parallels between wives of clergy and husbands of clergy are difficult to draw for several reasons:

1. Traditionally, women have been expected to work at home without pay while men have been expected to work outside the home to earn money to support the wife and family.

2. Women are more likely to have primary responsibilities for caring for children.

3. In the past, in a male-dominated church, women's groups in the church afforded women opportunity for relatively independent leadership, while men could attain leadership roles on the church's official boards and committees.

4. Because having men in authority has been the expected norm, some people may experience more difficulty seeing a woman in authority while her husband functions in roles appearing to have less authority or power.

These factors are changing in many churches and for many couples. Since men usually work for pay, married women clergy are automatically involved in a dual-career marriage, the topic of chapter 8. In addition to dual-career issues, the following factors are important for husbands of ministers:

1. Participation in sharing household responsibilities

2. Ability and willingness to adjust daily and weekly schedules in relation to the schedule of the pastor-wife

3. Skills and willingness to share parenting tasks if the couple has children

4. Ability to affirm his pastor-wife without being dominated by her or upstaging and overshadowing her

5. Comfortableness with his wife's autonomy, professional accomplishments, and commitment to her work as an ordained minister

6. Willingness to change residence location when she changes her church assignment or call

7. Skill in dealing with parishioners for whom ordained women clergy are in some way problematic; realization that this may be due to the parishioner's unresolved family and authority issues and/or be related to the power networks in the local church or community

Probably many years will pass before ministers' wives and ministers' husbands experience the same issues concerning their involvement in the parish and with their clergy-spouse. Certainly many issues will overlap. The increasing presence of clergy-husbands can help society at large, and the church in particular, to observe and study which issues are really spouse-parish issues in contrast with those that stem from and are related to sexist, marriage, family, or personal concerns.

Chapter 8.
Dual Careers
in Clergy Life

Consider the dynamics and dilemmas in the following conversations of two dual-career couples in which one spouse is a pastor.

"Guess what!" exclaimed Brenda, a successful accountant, to her husband, Ken. "The big promotion is almost here! Mr. Ridgely told me one of the senior partners is retiring next year. He said the firm wants to take a woman in as a senior partner, and that I, your ever-lovin' wife, am their first choice! One more year, and I'll be a real senior partner. The partners are meeting next week to make the offer official. I've dreamed of this ever since I started with the firm."

"That's great," confirmed Ken, now in his seventh year as pastor of All Saints' Church. "I'm really pleased for you. I just hope I can hold on at the church long enough for you to enjoy that position."

"But we can't move now," Brenda replied, with a worried smile. "I know we have discussed this, but it just wouldn't be right to leave an offer that I'll probably never get again. And the salary . . . well, as a senior partner, salary and commissions will just about double my current income. In fact, you would not need to work at all if you didn't want to."

In nearby suburb, Ann is completing her third year as associate minister at St. James Church. After getting their children to bed, she and her husband sit on the couch in their den discussing a call she has received to become pastor of a church two hundred miles away.

"My interview with the selection committee went really well," Ann continued, as Bob pulled her closer. "They were impressed with my work with senior citizens, and they want me to emphasize the very things I would like to do—visiting prospective members, improving the worship services, and developing the church school program."

"I'm glad you're excited about the offer," replied Bob. "I also have an offer I like very much. Since Dave plans to retire in three months, the head office wants me to take over as regional manager here. With fifty employees, there's no chance they will relocate the office."

Ann sat up quickly. "I agreed to stay here for these past eight years because of your work. I hope you will move with me if St. Luke's Church decides to call me as their pastor."

"Wait a minute." Slowly Bob sipped his coffee. "I do want to affirm your work for the Lord and your career. I also want this promotion very much. Maybe we could buy an airplane and commute to work."

"Bob, be serious! This is my calling."

"Yes, and my work is also my vocation in the Lord," Bob replied.

Perhaps in the silence some possible answers will emerge for Brenda and Ken and for Ann and Bob. What might they be? If you have a spouse who also is involved in a career, together read these vignettes and discuss how they may relate to your situation.

Both conversations illustrate some of the issues involved in a two-career couple. In *Ministry and Marriage*, Joan Hunt and Richard Hunt consider the range of dual-career couples in which at least one spouse is a pastor.[1] Their findings help in understanding some of the dynamics at work when couples are simultaneously pursuing professional ministry and nonministry careers.

Ministers in Dual-Careers

Dual-career marriages in which one spouse is clergy have special characteristics. If the clergyperson is a pastor, he or she has high visibility in the community. In large urban areas, the spouse may work outside the area in which the clergy-spouse is well known and may be relatively unaffected by actions of the pastor-spouse. In other instances, an unpopular stand or activity by the pastor-spouse may also affect the career standing and options of the other spouse. These influences may be moderated considerably if the clergy-spouse is less well known because of involvement in specialized ministries.

Clergy have work schedules spanning days and evenings of every day of the week, in addition to being subject to emergencies and other unexpected time demands. When the spouse is in a career (such as medicine or public service) that also has emergency requirements or unplanned interruptions, having time as a couple may be especially difficult to arrange.

In most denominations, it is unusual for clergy to be in the same community for most of their lives. For many pastors, a move every four to eight years is typical. Some careers, such as public school teaching or accounting, are more "portable," since similar positions are available in nearly every community. Even here, however, requirements for tenure and vestment in retirement plans may require a teacher to stay in the same school system a minimum number of years. Additionally, the greater availability of qualified teachers today often makes it difficult for newcomers to a community, including a pastor's spouse, to easily find a desirable position.

Some careers may depend upon the individual becoming established in a community and staying there for many years. Starting a business or professional practice are examples. In some instances, this is solved by the clergy-spouse being able to move from one pastorate to another in the same geographical area. More often, however, when the clergy-spouse is required to move, the other spouse faces the difficult question of whether to change career locations or leave the marriage.

Does Job = Career = Vocation?

We will use the word *career* to refer to the range of jobs, positions, and paid work through which an individual finds personal meaning and financial rewards.

Usually *job* or *position* refers to receiving pay from someone to do specified work. *Career* usually refers to a lifelong (at least extended) path of work, including a sequence of jobs, titles, or positions, that a person does and in which the individual feels much personal involvement. The root meaning of *vocation*, like *voice* and *vocal*, means "to call or express." From a Christian perspective, every person is called by God to useful work in the world as an expression of one's response to God.

Subjectively, an individual may make a career out of any type of work, paid or not. The key elements in career are these:

1. The work is a central and consistent factor in one's self-identity.

2. One receives a personal sense of self-esteem from doing the work.

3. One develops and maintains marketable skills in the chosen field of work.

4. There is some degree of self-direction and choice about which jobs one will accept.

Francine Hall and Douglas Hall differentiate between traditional career and *protean* career perspectives[2] They characterize these views as the "work ethic" and the "worth ethic." As a society, they suggest, we are moving away from the old Protestant work ethic. According to the Halls' interpretation, this ethic emphasized work as a way to salvation and protection against temptation. It valued pay, security, status, and company loyalty.

In contrast, the modern "worth ethic" emphasizes personal satisfaction in a role of one's choice, self-definition of goals and values to be gained from a career, personal values as criteria for success, and the individual's control over one's career definition and directions.

The Halls' term *protean* is taken from the Greek god of the sea, Proteus, who could change to any form in order to ensure his survival and dominance. In the protean couple, spouses are individuals capable of shaping both their careers and marriage to accomplish the goals they value for themselves. Although realistically responsive to work requirements, in the final analysis it is the spouses, not the employer or work setting, who determine the worth of their work in relation to their own goals and values.

Career Stages

The lifetime career cycle, described in chapter 11, interacts with issues facing the two-career couple. In each year of one's life, the question of whether the next step is advancement, maintenance, or decline is open. At times, one may maintain a pastorate, or perhaps serve in what appears as a declining position, in order to advance subsequently to a different church.

Especially for clergy, the length of each of these stages depends heavily upon one's competence, interests, energy, health, and opportunities. An individual's personal, inner perspective may or may not match the external perspective of others in deciding where one is in this career cycle. A person's standard for success, as will be noted in chapter 10, entitled "Ministerial Effectiveness," greatly affects where one places oneself in these stages.

Individual, Marriage, and Family Stages

Career stages interact with the individual, marriage, and family stages of two-career couples. Issues facing two-career couples are heavily influenced by where each partner is in his or her own life journey and where they are as a couple in their marriage relationship. Too often the concept of family stages, based on the ages of the children (usually the age of the oldest child), overshadows the important personal development of the spouses as individuals and as partners.

Concepts of adult development come from many sources. For example, Eric Erikson[3] and Daniel Levinson[4] describe some of the issues and transitions across the adult life span. Career stages tend to interact with these personal development issues in ways that are far too extensive to consider in this chapter.

Dual-career decisions also trigger other issues between spouses. Some of these are the quality of love and care each partner expresses to the other and receives from the partner. Unresolved relationships with parents, siblings, or other family-of-origin members may involve expectations, control, anger, or loss, and these may be indirectly expressed in issues relating to two-career problems or concerns. Among many resources for considering these dimensions of marriage are the social learning, cognitive, family systems, psychoanalytic, and family-of-origin perspectives presented in works by T.J. Paolino and B.S. McCrady,[5] and Neil S. Jacobson and Alan S. Gurman.[6]

Clergy, especially those in two-career marriages, can benefit from considering how relationship issues with their own parents and siblings, their spouse's relatives, and their children, whether biologically related or adopted, become intermixed with church administration and pastoral care issues. Edwin H. Friedman covers these issues in his study on family and church systems.[7]

Younger Couples: Career, Marriage, and Family

Couples in their twenties and thirties are typically in the early entry and advancement stages of career development, as well as being in their early years of marriage. In addition, having younger children may further complicate their career decisions. These couples may face issues such as the following:[8]

1. Similar career demands, such as travel, relocation, long hours, and heavy investment of time and energy in proving oneself on the job, whether church or other setting

2. Conflicting career choices and options because job opportunities may not come to each partner at the same time and in the same locality

3. Intense commitment to career because both partners want to succeed in their careers

4. Lack of preparedness to cope with the stresses of managing a home, two careers, and having younger children

5. Less experience in managing conflict between themselves in the context of being committed to each other in marriage

6. Hesitation to discuss options with the church leaders or corporate managers because of fear of the organization or employer

For some couples, a conflict about career options may be the first major conflict they have experienced in their marriage. "My career/life vs. yours" may also indirectly express expectations or ties to parents and family expectations. Pressures to succeed, whether from self or others, may further intensify the need to place one's own career ahead of anything or anyone else.

A younger couple can take several steps to reduce the influence of these factors. First, take a long-range view of both partners' careers in relation to the marriage, children, and other life goals. Talking about the next ten to fifteen years can enable a couple to place a better perspective on career preparation and entry-level choices they must make. This will take a unique pattern for each couple.

Some couples may plan for the wife to complete her career preparation, work two or three years, take some time out for having children, and then return to work as the children become older. Other couples may want children first, after which the wife will continue her career. Some couples share parenting; in this arrangement, each spouse takes about the same amount of time from career while the children are younger.

If one or both careers require frequent moves, the spouses may agree that (1) one partner will be willing to move with the other partner for a certain number of years, and (2) after this period of time they will be "settled" by a given age. Some couples may agree that they will have to live apart for some weeks out of the year because of career demands.

Second, take a medium-range view (such as several months or more) of schedules relating to careers, marriage, and church activities. Anticipate heavy, hectic weeks and plan for more time together as a couple in other nearby weeks that have less pressure. For example, Advent/Christmas, Lent/Easter, and church budget /canvas times may be especially busy for a pastor, while the spouse in the nonparish career may be busier at end of month, tax time, or other seasons of the career. By anticipating these, a couple can realize the extra pressures each may have, recognize their greater vulnerabilities, and plan ways to give increased support to each other during these times.

Third, take a short-range view (such as the weekly cycle). One spouse may be busier at certain periods during each week. The other spouse may then plan to do more of the housework during these times. On the days when both spouses are busy and more tired, eating out may be the best solution to preparing the evening meal. On days when one spouse is more likely to be tired, the other spouse may do all or most of meal preparation and cleanup. Many variations on these possibilities allow each couple to be in charge of their lives and create constructive patterns for both careers and marriage.

For ministers in a local parish, it is also important for the spouses to agree on how much the nonclergy spouse will be involved in parish activities. Most couples today assume that the nonclergy spouse is not hired as an "unpaid associate pastor" with the spouse who is pastor. Together the couple will need to communicate this agreement to the local church leaders.

For flexibility to work, both partners must be confident that she or he will not "lose out" by allowing the other to go first. Sometimes a couple initially agrees that the husband will complete his career preparation first while the wife earns money to support the family; subsequently, the wife will do her major career preparation while the husband provides financially for the family.

This may go sour after the husband completes his preparation and then "forgets" or disagrees with the wife's desire to do her equivalent preparation. When this happens, the wife feels that her husband has taken advantage of her willingness to invest heavily in his career with the hope of a delayed payoff years later. In some cases, divorce my result, and the jilted wife may then sue her former husband successfully to obtain some reimbursement for time and energy she put into his career. Once again, mutual trust between partners is essential in these longer-range agreements and perspectives.

Mid-Life Couples: Career, Marriage, and Family

Several factors may benefit couples in their later thirties and forties as they manage marriage, two careers, and a family.[9]

1. As one becomes deeply established in a career, mobility may lessen. Alternately, because of life experience (paid work, volunteer, or hobby skills), partners may have more options and more confidence for trying new or atypical arrangements in combining marriage, family, and careers.

2. Individual, couple, and family goals may be much clearer. Thus, partners may be more able to agree on priorities in career choices.

3. Some family goals, such as getting the children through high school and college, may be much closer to completion. The couple may have more financial stability through higher salaries, savings, and home equity but may also have heaviest debts because of illness, accidents, responsibilities for aging parents, or other concerns.

4. Each partner may be more able to empathize with the other concerning demands and possibilities, yet may also continue to be highly committed to her or his own career.

5. Individuals may have greater confidence in negotiating with employers about job requirements in relation to marriage and family priorities. In some instances, the mid-life individual may be in a management or other position that gives more control over his or her choices.

6. Because they have solved earlier conflicts, mid-life people have greater skills for negotiating issues, creating solutions, and implementing them.

7. The career successes and failures of each spouse may be less threatening to the marriage and family because both partners have many other reasons to continue to be with each other. Greater confidence in the marriage relationship may also enable spouses to accept temporary times of living apart because of careers, public recognition of the other's career accomplishments, and more possibilities for vacations and pre-retirement planning.

8. Other life values may become more important than specific career advancement or accomplishments.

Clergy Couples

Clergy couples are a special instance of two-career marriages. As with other couples the relationship has certain advantages and disadvantages. The term *clergy couple* usually refers to the special two-career couple in which both partners are ordained ministers. An estimated 1 to 2 percent of over three hundred thousand Protestant clergy have spouses who are also clergy. Thus, there are perhaps four thousand clergy couples in the United States today.

In addition, in many couples, one spouse is an ordained minister and the other spouse has a career within a church structure, such as being a Christian education director, child-care worker, church secretary, musician, or counselor.

A major advantage of a clergy couple is that both spouses are trained in the same career field. This opens the possibility for them to serve in the same church with the same, or similar, work settings. This can permit both spouses to have similar interests, schedules, and opportunities.

On the other hand, there are possible disadvantages when both spouses are ordained ministers. With similar skills and training, it is much easier for others, and perhaps the spouses also, to compare the two as professionals, with one spouse inevitably being judged as somewhat more competent than the other. In some couples, resentment may develop. This can increase competition between the partners, or it may subtly encourage the less competent spouse to be more dependent on the more successful one.

If the spouses serve in different churches, not only are schedules likely to conflict on weekends and evenings, but it is difficult for each spouse to participate only as "spouse" in the other partner's professional life and activities.

Career conflicts experienced as difficulties for some couples become opportunities for others. Several factors can enable clergy couples, as well as other two-career couples, to succeed in their marriage as they also succeed in their careers.[10]

What Makes Dual-Careers Work

At any age, the following suggestions can enable spouses to succeed in their marriage and in their careers.

1. Both partners are committed to each other and support each other regardless of who has which career.

2. Competition between partners is resolved and minimized because each partner is confident of self and each partner affirms the other.

3. Partners share the daily tasks of homemaking according to their interests, time schedules, and available energy.

4. Both partners realize that, at times, each person's career must take priority over the other, but over the long run these either balance out or otherwise fit the expectations and values of both partners.

5. Where children are involved, appropriate child care is available and used. Partners agree on who will be available in emergencies and for unexpected needs of the children.

6. Partners place their commitment to each other ahead of their careers.

7. Partners are secure enough with each other that the salary, prestige, and other statuses of each career are not used to "put down" the other partner.

8. Partners have career positions that permit them to exert at least partial control over their own work schedules.

9. Partners plan some personal time, couple time, and family time every week or on some other regular schedule agreeable to both. When work demands usurp this time in a given week, spouses agree on compensatory "make-up" activities in other weeks.

10. Partners are relatively free from needs to prove themselves in their careers, unconscious needs to dominate the other partner, and fears of losing the partner to work or to a possible romantic involvement with work associates.

11. Partners agree on standards of career success for themselves and each other.

12. Partners have established methods for deciding about promotions, relocation moves related to the career, use of income from each career, and related issues.

13. Partners agree on how much each will be involved in job-related social functions and other activities that in some way benefit the career of the other spouse.

Individual and Work-Place Factors

The success of dual-career couples is partly in themselves and partly in the conditions of their careers. Success in marriage and career requires that each partner is able to (1) function as an autonomous person, (2) give affection and care to their partner, and (3) receive affection from their partner. In addition, each partner must have sufficient preparation and skill to be successful in their chosen career area.

If one partner is more successful than the other, according to standards held by both partners, it may be more difficult for each to deal with the imbalanced success. The successful partner may chide the other for not succeeding and thereby create resentment on both sides. In other instances, the more successful one may redouble efforts to help the other partner, which reduces the time available for his or her own career. The less successful partner may become discouraged, resentful, or act out feelings of failure or anger in other ways.

The couple's desired standard of living also affects their career options. A couple in debt and with heavy financial commitments will feel much more pressure to make career decisions based on income from the work. At the other extreme, some couples save a substantial portion of their moderate combined income because they do not spend much on anything other than basic needs.

The more control each individual has over his or her work schedule, the more the couple can be sure that their plans can actually be completed. If a congregation demands that the pastor is never away on any Sunday in the year and is also at the church every day during the week, many possibilities for the couple are eliminated. If the nonclergy spouse has a job setting with assigned hours that cannot be modified easily, this will also eliminate many options for the couple to be creatively flexible in arranging career and marriage.

Higher income and lower financial indebtedness provide greater flexibility for a couple in deciding that one spouse will not work outside the home. Couples who barely survive on both paychecks are much less able to consider the possibility of one spouse not working for an extended period of time. It is, therefore, wise to plan carefully and make financial decisions that benefit each spouse both in the short-range and the long-range.

Demand for the skills of each spouse also affects career choices. Even though an individual is highly qualified, a job market that does not value those abilities reduces the options of the couple for career plans. Developing a variety of interests and skills, and updating these on a regular basis, will enable couples to effectively manage the challenges of balancing career and home relationships.

Chapter 9.
Staff Relationships in Ministry

Clergy staff relationships differ in each situation. For example, consider the case of Tom Giddings, the new senior minister of a Presbyterian church in southern California.

This is what Tom said about the pastor whose associate he was before he came to his new church: "He's the pastor of the largest church in the presbytery. I was his associate for five years before becoming senior pastor of my present church. I never got to know him well. We went our separate ways, performed our assigned duties, met together occasionally, but that was about all. I wasn't sure he cared much for me. Seemingly, he was only interested in how well I did the tasks he delegated to me. It was a lonely time. I decided to seek my own church. At least there I wouldn't expect a relationship. I'd be by myself."

The canon at the Cathedral of St. Stephen had quite a different experience during his twenty years as a member of the cathedral staff. When a new dean of the cathedral arrived, one of the canon's friends asked him if he was uneasy about having a new boss. He replied, "In my years at this cathedral, I have served under three deans. I expect to be affirmed by the new dean, Benjamin Proxmire, as much as by the others. I'll do a good job *with* him and *for* him. I look forward to his coming. He will help me fulfill my ministry, and I will assist him in his."

The experience of these two assistants was radically different. One felt isolated, alone, and unfulfilled. The other felt accepted, supported, and affirmed. These reports are fairly typical of what many staff members report. Unfortunately, far too many experiences are the type reported by Tom Giddings rather than the one told by the canon at the Cathedral of St. Stephen.

Although Giddings stayed four years, one report noted that the average tenure for staff assistants was less than fifteen months.[1] According to one church consultant, "the overwhelming majority of associate staff members are frustrated and often angry. Serving as a staff member can be the most painful position in ministry."[2]

Mitchell conducted over 350 conversations with clergy and their assistants. His judgments about the state of affairs among church staff are probably as current today as when he made them more than two decades ago. He stated, "Relationships within the multiple staff ministry seem to be relatively unstable. There is a rapid turnover of assistant pastors. There are constant reports of clashes between ministers."[3] The vast majority of Mitchell's sample felt a great need for determining what makes for good staff relationships.

This chapter will describe some of the processes that enhance relationships among clergy staff. Prior to doing this, however, we will review several features unique to the experience of ordained clergypersons. These features pertain to (1) the motivation for becoming religious professionals, (2) a broad understanding of the clergy role, and (3) the psychodynamics of staff relationships.

Clergy Motivation

The first feature to remember is that individuals who become ordained clergy have unique needs and impulses. Typically, they report feeling "called" to enter the ministry. This means they have a sense of being summoned by Almighty God to be one of his ordained clergy.

While it may be a Christian ideal that all people view their vocations as if they are doing what God intends them to do, it is rare for laypersons to talk about themselves as being "called by God." The "priesthood of all believers" is still not a reality for most people; in this regard, however, what is rare for the average Christian is the *norm* for ministers.

The authors often participate on candidate selection committees in a large mainline denomination known for its sophisticated and highly educated clergy. One might think this denomination would have outgrown the idea that people are called by God to a given vocation. It might be presumed that to think God selected a specific vocation for an individual would be as preposterous as suggesting that God selected a given person to be one's spouse. Yet even here, the first thing said to each candidate during the interview is, "Tell us about your call to ministry." This sophisticated denomination still expects that its clergy will have the unique sense that they are chosen by God to do the work of ministry. This type of motivation is even more typical in other denominations.

The sense of divine election lends an air of urgency and ultimacy to whatever position a given clergyperson may occupy at a particular time. Any suggestion that a youth minister, for example, is not taking his or her job seriously enough is likely to be an error. Usually, clergy take their job and themselves *too* seriously. This is sometimes difficult for parish officials to understand when a minister seems to make a mistake of judgment or appears to be uninvolved in a certain role.

Think back to the story of David, the Evangelical Lutheran Church pastor mentioned in chapter 2, who told of writing a theme for an English class in college entitled "My Call to Ministry." The professor suggested he change the title to "My Decision to Enter Ministry." She simply could not understand the concept of a "call" and felt the young student was being messianic. Obviously, the professor simply did not know much about clergy motivation.

Yet, even when the Theological School Inventory assesses "natural" as distinguished from "special" leading, it presumes that candidates taking this test will feel, in some spiritual way, that God has (1) acted to help them evaluate their "natural" abilities and gifts, and (2) enabled them, as a result of completing the evaluation, to reach a decision to enter ministry just as surely as if God had spoken to them in some special way apart from any rational process.

Thus, for most ministers, the position they occupy at a given time is not just a job; it is the channel through which they fulfill their calling. As such, they often feel unsuccessful unless major change is occurring in the lives of those with whom they work. They become easily discouraged and are frequently inner-directed. This may lead them to seek little advice and to act unilaterally. Underneath the surface, they are deeply involved in their work.

This unique type of motivation has important implications for staff relationships. Senior pastors, as well as laypersons, tend to forget their staff are motivated in this fashion. Sometimes senior pastors use clergy staff to do tasks for which the head of staff no longer has an interest or about which he or she feels over-burdened. In so doing, they, like the pastor under whom Tom Giddings served, fail to ask the important question, Do you feel you are fulfilling your calling in the work you do? Too often senior pastors seem interested only in getting the job done and not being bothered. Staff clergy rely heavily on the affirmation and interest of their superiors. They yearn for approval and concern. This is an inordinate need based on the sense that a transcendent power has called them to this role.

A Broad Understanding of Ministry

Another feature of clergy careers pertains to a broad, rather than a narrow, understanding of ministry. A narrow definition of ministry usually centers on the specific task to be performed: youth work, parish visitation, service to the homeless, evangelism, or preaching. A broad definition of ministry focuses on the mission of the church and the role of clergy as they serve that mission through a variety of functions. Most ministers envision themselves as wanting to be "in ministry" within all these varied channels. They have a *broad* rather than a *narrow* view of their career.

Clergy are not satisfied for long in roles that limit their function. Shawchuck estimates that youth pastors, for example, last only eighteen months on the average.[4] The canon who had served at the Cathedral of St. Stephen for twenty years was an exception to this rule. Even here, however, our guess is that the openness of the deans to allow the canon to participate in all functions of the full ministry made those twenty years so fulfilling.

It is unusual for a clergy staff member to remain willingly in a confined role for long if he or she does not have these "broader" opportunities. Most ministers desire to become a senior pastor, and this desire is most often based on a need to be involved in all facets of the task. While nonordained staff members, such as organists and church business administrators, may not feel this same imperative, ordained clergy are characterized by this urge toward a broad perspective.

This desire for the opportunity to function broadly is somewhat unique to ordained clergy. Although an increasing number of graduates from the nation's schools of business desire to be general managers or CEOs (chief executive officers) with broad responsibilities, the more typical graduate seems content with more narrow responsibilities in fields such as accounting, purchasing, marketing, or production. The exception for business school graduates is the norm for ordained clergy. They feel called to the total task of ministry—not just a given staff position.

If senior ministers desire to increase cohesion and enhance performance among their ordained staff, they will vigilantly provide opportunities for their clergy subordinates to participate in all facets of ministry. Senior pastors, however, tend to resist doing this, as the example of Tom Giddings, with which this chapter began, illustrates. Senior clergy are busy with the tasks for which they have *major* responsibility and have little energy left to worry about whether their clergy staff would like to share some of these duties. Asking senior ministers to concern themselves about providing opportunities for staff to do tasks other than those for which these associates were hired in the first place may suggest a confusion of roles and a waste of time and effort.

Yet, this is where ministry is unique. Attending to a broader understanding of ministry and giving the youth worker, for example, a chance to do hospital visiting, evangelism, and even preaching will pay significant dividends in staff longevity and effectiveness. More than one in four of Mitchell's informants said they thought each staff member should have opportunities to serve as a "full minister" even though their job descriptions gave them responsibility for only one or two areas.

Senior ministers who make the full range of opportunities available and who explain these actions to church officers report that junior members of the staff greatly appreciate these chances to develop their ministry skills. Their performance improves, rather than detracts from, their more specific responsibilities. When this process is explained to laypersons, they understand and feel integrally involved in the development of the *full* ministry of the staff, even though they may recognize that certain staff members do certain things better than others—preaching, for example. Shawchuck candidly concludes;

> Much of the responsibility lies with the senior minister. . . . While it is true that one person alone can't create good staff morale, only the senior pastor can block the efforts of others to do so. When it comes to staff climate and maturation, the senior minister functions either like a channel through which attitudes and resources flow, or like a cork in a bottle that restricts the flow.[5]

Likewise, Mitchell makes the sharing of all the roles of ministry one of his cardinal rules for enhancing staff relationships. He suggests that good staff functioning includes provision "for the regular exercise of its members of *all* the necessary leadership functions."[6]

We have often been asked, How can I motivate my staff? This question is usually asked by those who do not realize that their staffs are already highly motivated; under the constraints of their job assignments, however, they may have become lethargic and resigned. They do not lack motivation. They lack opportunity. After all, they believe they have been "called by God" to this role; ministry is their destiny.

Thus, the proper question is, How can I help *motivated* staff to act? rather than, How can I motivate my staff? One answer to this question is, Recognize that staff are looking for channels through which to express their calling. Open the way for them. Share *all* the roles. Do not confine your staff to a narrow definition of ministry.

The Psychodynamics of Staff Relationships

This leads to a third feature of clergy experience, namely, the feelings of ambivalence that permeate staff interaction. *Ambivalence* is the term for "a mixture of the feelings of love and hate." It is the natural essence of staff psychodynamics. While these ambivalent or contradictory feelings may be inherent among all staffs—whether in business or in the church—they are accentuated among ministers. This is due, in part, to the aforementioned messianic sense among clergy that they have been called by God to fill this particular life role.

Junior clergy often experience a mixture of feelings about the senior pastor under whom they work: like and dislike; affirmation and disapproval; trust and fear; confiding in and hiding from; even love and hate. A sense of precarious dependency exists that permeates the relationship. And what is even more striking is that senior clergy often feel these same emotions! While they appreciate the assistance that junior staff give them in ministry, they often fear the associates under them will mutiny against their leadership or sabotage their plans. Like their junior colleagues, they trust, yet fear, the staff who share their ministry. They feel their own calling is constantly in danger.

Fortunately, the balance of these ambivalent feelings is most frequently toward the positive emotions. Most of the time, staff maintain enough trust, love, and affirmation toward each other to provide a semblance of good functioning. But negative, distrustful, and fearful feelings are just beneath the surface and have the potential of erupting at any time.

The overwhelming dependency that staff have on each other for the success of their ministries is the key to why this ambivalence is such a dominant feature of the psychodynamics of church staff relationships. When the balance shifts, conflict and projection of blame often result.

A denomination's district minister recently told us the following story, which illustrates what can happen when ambivalence in staff relationships gets out of hand.

One Monday morning I received a call from an officer in one of our churches about fifty miles north of my office. "The president of the congregation and I would like to meet you for lunch," he said. "We have a problem in our staff."

Later that week I met them at a restaurant midway between the church and my office. They reported that the two ministers of their church were not getting along, and this was becoming a major problem in the congregation. They said that the ministers openly contradicted each other in public, gossiped about each other to church members, failed to support each others' programs, and acted as if each other were not present in board meetings. The officers were very worried about the bad example the two ministers regularly set before the congregation.

I told them I would see what I could do. I phoned each of the pastors and asked him to come to my office for an interview. Each pastor spoke negatively about the other and insisted the problems of the church could be solved if the other one changed his ways or left the church. Neither took the blame for any of the dissent observed by the officers. They blamed the other pastor entirely.

I asked each minister to meet together with me. I told them to stop acting like little boys. I faced them with the way in which their interdependency was unwittingly leading them toward negative feelings. I affirmed each of their calls to ministry and encouraged them to face the underlying dynamics causing their trouble. I assured them that this was fairly natural for clergy, but that it had to be acknowledged or it would destroy their ministries. I did not try to make them "forgive and forget" their differences but face them and live with them.

So far, I think my counsel to them is working. It's been six months, and I have had no further calls from their officers.

This story illustrates how unadmitted ambivalence can infiltrate clergy relations and cause great conflict that disillusions parish members. It also shows the power of admitting that ambivalence exists and that it is understandable. Church staff relations are inherently ambivalent because interdependency is so great.

If ambivalence is denied or projected onto others' foibles, it can destroy a staff. If it is acknowledged and managed, it can be a strengthening factor. Mitchell includes handling these mixed feelings among his cardinal recommendations for increasing cohesion among clergy. He states, "Negative aspects of staff relationships should be appropriately dealt with. Open acknowledgement, clear delineation of issues, and attempts at repair and reconciliation should be made."[7]

Effective Church Staffs

Having considered these basic features, let us now turn to three characteristics we have found in effective church staffs that enhance their relationships: (1) responsibility with freedom, (2) evaluation with support, and (3) relationship without socializing.

Responsibility with Freedom

The first characteristic of effective church staffs is that each member is given "responsibility with freedom." This means that every person is assigned a given area of responsibility, such as children, families, social service, missions, or evangelism. But it also means that each individual has the freedom to fulfill that responsibility in whatever way she or he sees fit.

One person wrote about his experience on such a staff:

> I was invited to take a position with the Dakotas Area Program staff of the United Methodist Church. I met with the other two staff members to establish priorities and assign responsibilities. After two days of hammering out specifics, we listed the necessary staff functions and assigned positions to each of us based on our interests, time, and skills.
>
> Following this, we each developed objectives and programs within our areas of responsibility, submitted them to each other for review, revision, and approval, and then set about to carry out the programs as we saw fit. . . .
>
> Bob Paul was director of the staff, but he functioned as a team member. Ron and he voiced strong ideas about what I should do in management areas. But not once in the years we worked together did they move into my areas of freedom unless I asked them to. I always felt fully supported, never abandoned, and I knew I was responsible for the success or failure of my areas.[8]

The staff member had responsibility with freedom. *Poor* staff relationships are characterized by the reverse of this dictum, namely, "ambiguity without authority." In his classic survey, Mitchell found that over one-fifth of the church staff members reported a great need for job analyses.[9] Thus, a significant percentage of his informants were unclear about their responsibilities. The interesting thing is that, in many of these cases, staff members were given little authority to act even if they had known what they were expected to do!

There are two facets to the "responsibility with freedom" recommendation. If "ambiguity without authority" is to be avoided, clear job descriptions must be formulated, on the one hand, and, on the other hand, opportunities to pursue those tasks with great latitude must be afforded.

Formulating clear job descriptions with specific assigned areas of responsibility may seem the opposite of our earlier recommendation that each ordained church staff member be given the opportunity to perform all the tasks of ministry. Being a full minister and having limited assignments may seem contradictory. At best, however, these two elements work as complements to each other rather than opposites.

Distinguishing between "regular" and "occasional" tasks will help to clarify the possibility that specific duties need not conflict with a broad understanding of ministry. Regular tasks are those areas of ministry for which one has primary responsibility. Occasional tasks are those areas of ministry for which one has secondary responsibility.

As stated earlier, senior clergy need to share their regular duties occasionally with junior staff. This idea is based on a presupposition that senior pastors usually perform the more glamorous tasks, such as the liturgical, sacramental, and preaching roles. The reverse is also true, however. Junior staff need to make a concerted effort to involve senior clergy in tasks the head of staff may have given up but may occasionally yearn to perform, such as visitation, youth work, and evangelism. Both senior and junior staff have a responsibility here.

This obligation for periodic involvement of others in all the tasks of ministry is based on each staff member having an area of responsibility over which he or she has control and authority. Specific aspects of ministry, such as family life, Bible study, and administration, will not be successfully accomplished—much less shared among the staff—unless specific staff persons have primary responsibility for them.

Broad ministerial sharing can, therefore, be coupled with narrow job assignments. The two need not contradict each other. In fact, they are dependent upon one another. We have seen mistakes made both ways. On the one hand, staff members are sometimes employed to do specific tasks but never have opportunities to participate in other areas of church life. More typically, clergy have been employed as "associates" rather than "assistants" and are told in an idealistic manner, "I want you to be my co-pastor and to share all areas of ministry with me." In this latter case, new staff members have no idea what their specific duties are and the relationship quickly deteriorates and becomes competitive.

As one might have guessed, we do not recommend hiring "associates." We recommend employing "assistants." There has to be a structure to the staff with clear lines of authority. This does not mean that leadership and decision making cannot be shared, as Shawchuck illustrated in his example noted above. It does mean that clergy are peculiarly susceptible to thinking idealistically rather than structurally. One rector we know became so excited about the addition of a female assistant to his parish that he promised her participation in every facet of the church's life within the first three months. This led to over-expectation on her part and great confusion among the members. She would have been perfectly satisfied to minister as an "assistant" rather that an "associate." Had this happened she would have been happier, and the relationship would not have broken apart in nine months!

Clear job descriptions must be formulated. These need to include specific tasks each staff member is expected to perform coupled with general areas of ministry over which the staff member has responsibility. For example, if a person is employed as director of Christian education, the job description should include statements such as these:

> *Specific duties:* unlock the church on Sunday mornings 30 minutes before church school begins.

> *General area:* plan and direct a program for adult Christian education.

After staff have agreed on the responsibilities of the job description, great latitude needs to be given in the accomplishment of those responsibilities.This is what is meant by "responsibility with freedom." Freedom does not mean irresponsibility. Staff members cannot claim that their freedom has been violated if they fail to fulfill specific duties they agreed to perform, such as unlocking the church on Sunday mornings at a certain time. Freedom pertains to the opportunity to use one's own style and priorities in leading the church within those broad areas of church life for which one has assumed responsibility, such as adult Christian education.

Giving staff this kind of freedom is easier said than done on the part of senior ministers because they have ambivalent feelings about their staff. This is understandable. As Harry Truman stated, "The buck stops here." Senior pastors are held responsible for the effective functioning of their staff. Staff members can make or break senior clergy. Senior ministers receive pressure from laypersons who may disapprove of the performance of staff and from staff members who may perform their duties very idiosyncratically.

Two aspects of freedom are especially important for good staff relations. The first is style and the second is communication. Style refers to the *way* a task is performed rather than *what* is performed. Agreement needs to be reached about the style with which a given staff member will function. Unfortunately, most job descriptions focus on *what* is to be done but neglect to state *how* it should be done. This may sound like a curtailment of freedom, but it is not meant to be so.

Most staff disagreements occur over style or how a job is performed. Helpful tools are available to enable leaders and staff members in becoming aware of their expectations regarding style. One of these is the *Job/Person/Match* scale, which assesses characteristics such as a person's preference for a way of making decisions, autonomy, leading, and controlling, as well as the individual's desire to be in contact with people, the number and variety of tasks with which one feels comfortable at a given time, feedback on performance, and involvement in service to others.

These are all stylistic variables. Both senior and junior ministers should complete a scale like this to determine if the newcomer's way of accomplishing tasks generally match the preferences of the supervisor's for the way things should be done. Where there are differences, negotiations can take place before the new staff member is employed. Where there is agreement on style, there will be cooperation and cohesion. Where the differences are too apparent, great caution should be taken in hiring the staff member. When styles match, responsibility with freedom is possible. The senior clergyperson will trust the subordinate to do whatever is done in a way that does not offend and can be supported.

The other aspect of the relationship that makes responsibility with freedom possible is communication. One cardinal rule of staff relationships is, Never let the boss be surprised. It is always better if one's superior knows ahead of time if there is to be any novel way of doing something. For example, if the youth group plans to have a square dance, and even the slightest possibility exists that someone will complain, the youth pastor should tell the senior pastor before the dance occurs. Senior pastors should hear information first from their staff—not from church members.

When senior pastors know what to expect, they are far less likely to disapprove of an event. They will usually support the staff if they are not caught off guard. Moreover, it is always wise to elicit the support of one's superiors. This is especially true in a voluntary organization where total support for any activity is never possible. There will usually be some complaints. However, if staff meetings have included open discussion of upcoming events and free expression of opinions, the senior pastor will more likely give support when criticism arises.

It is important for senior clergy to remember, however, that communication must be two-way. If staff members are expected to inform, senior pastors should be expected to respond. If the head of staff intends to oppose a staff decision when church members complain, the junior staff should be made aware of this. Again, keep surprises to a minimum. Good communication is the name of the game in "responsibility with freedom."

Evaluation with Support

The next key to effective church staff relationships is "evaluation with support." This means regular assessment of how well the staff is doing coupled with implicit as well as explicit affirmation.

An old maxim is essential to remember as the first step in assessing performance: "Criticize in private; affirm in public." Both are crucial. The locales are different, however. While it is impossible to totally support *everything* either a senior or junior clergyperson does, this maxim can be espoused in principle, and staff can confront each other if, and when, it is violated. In almost every long-lasting, cohesive staff with which we are acquainted, this understanding—that they will support each other in public and critique each other in private—is followed.

Our recommendation is that there be an explicit, even a written, agreement among staff members to this effect. Such an agreement should apply both up as well as down. This means that junior staff members will not engage in public criticism of the senior pastor. They will be loyal to him or her. Senior pastors should be able to count on the support of staff as much as the staff should be able to count on the support of superiors.

Two things happen when people are criticized in public rather than in private. First, they feel overexposed, embarrassed, and anxious. Second, when people feel these ways, they react by becoming self-justifying, combative, acquiescing, or depressed. None of these feelings lead to a constructive response to criticism, nor does this behavior build staff cohesion. As noted earlier, staff feel very vulnerable to the approval of their superiors. They overreact to public negative criticism and tend to become disheartened or hostile rather than interested in correcting their performance. This dynamic is as true for senior ministers as for their staff members.

There is one exception to the suggestion that public critique has adverse consequences: when the evaluation is positive rather than negative. For example, the pastor might compliment the minister of music by stating during the morning worship service, "The Christmas concert last Friday night was one of the most inspirational events I have ever experienced." The reaction of the minister of music will be 180 degrees different from that which might occur if the pastor had said, "Although there were mishaps and miscues, we had our traditional Christmas concert last Friday night. I wish more of you had attended."

Staff reaction to affirmations leave them feeling more confident, proud, and self-accepting. While such public compliments could be conceived as support rather than critique, compliments are, in fact, forms of evaluation. Criticism should be understood as both positive and negative. Better said, criticism should be both corrective and sustaining.

Clergy performance is rarely all good or all bad. Staff functioning, like all human behavior, exists "this side of heaven." It is never perfect, even though most clergy would like to presume so! Thus, there is always room for improvement—even when an event has been singularly successful. The reverse is also true; very few events are total failures.

If we assume that most, if not all, staff members are well motivated and feel called by God to their role, we will expect them to accept both positive and negative confirmation of their efforts. Church members and staff will realize that pastors, like all Christians, are sinners saved by grace through faith and, thus, everything they do could be improved.

Our judgment is that all critique should include commendations as well as recommendations. Additionally, commendation should precede recommendation. Staff should be honored for their best and helped to change their worst—in that order. If recommendations are to be truly heard and acted upon, they must be on a firm foundation of pride and affirmation. For example, a staff meeting might well begin with the senior clergyperson saying, "Let's look together at what we did this past month. Let's list our tasks and begin by reporting to each other what we liked about how things went. Let's commend each other for the jobs we have done."

Staff members should be cautioned, however, to make both the commendations and recommendations distinct and honest. Commendations should not be used in a manipulative manner, as, for example, when a staff member said, "I like the length of the sermon you preached last Sunday, but I couldn't understand what that story about the dog had to do with your point." In this case, the person seemed to be looking for something to compliment but was really intent on making the negative point about the dog story. Commendations and recommendations should be considered separately—not at the same time. Staff should feel affirmed about some genuinely good aspects of their performance.

The caution about not connecting negative criticism with positive criticism is related to a double problem we have observed in church staffs. On the one hand, senior ministers often feel so threatened and insecure that they can't see the good points in the performance of other members. Thus, their commendations are strained and manipulative. They are overly critical in a negative fashion. Their staffs never feel affirmed.

On the other hand, some senior ministers do not know how to give corrective recommendations. Instead of giving helpful critique, they presume that other staff cannot change. They tolerate each other and engage in denial, cynicism, or polyannish compliments. Because they feel powerless to change their staff, they criticize them behind their backs and are never honest in an open manner. Other senior pastors may idealize their staff and refuse to see any areas where they might improve, even when many in the congregation complain.

Staff evaluation should begin with commendations, followed by a coffee break. After this, the pastoral team should make recommendations to one another. This pattern will assure that suggestions for improving or correcting performance will be made against a secure sense of support and a good self-concept.

Returning to the maxim with which we began this discussion of "evaluation with support," remaining loyal to each other in public should not be confused with never being honest in evaluation. Recommendations for improvement should definitely be made, and people should be honest with each other, but this should be done face to face and away from the public eye. No member of a staff should ever hear, secondhand, a negative remark made about him or her by another staff person in another setting. Respect for the feelings of others, coupled with a commitment to honesty with one another, is the foundation of staff cohesion.

There are several other characteristics of evaluation with support. The first is that evaluation should be conducted in terms of an agreed-upon job description. The job description should include explicit statements about performance style as well as what one is expected to accomplish. When this is done, staff know what to expect. When an evaluation is conducted without such a job description, personal feelings get in the way.

The next characteristic of evaluation with support is that it should begin with *self*-evaluation. Staff should agree that this is the place where critique begins and that what people think about their own performance is taken with as much seriousness as what other staff members think. If agreement is reached on this procedure, people will not hesitate to give themselves commendations as well as recommendations.

Another characteristic of evaluation with support is that evaluation should occur at stated periods—not just at the end of a project. The experience of one minister to singles in a large church illustrates what happens when evaluation is not frequent enough. This staff member thought he was fulfilling his job description even though more singles who attended the meetings were working young adults rather than college-age youth. By looking at the church records, he noticed that more college youth had participated in the group before he joined the staff.

His immediate superior complimented the growth in the number of singles attending the programs, but there was no time when the staff officially evaluated his performance. In mid-March, he was called to a meeting with his superior, the director of Christian education, and the senior pastor. They pointed out that there had been some complaints from certain parents about his failure to minister adequately to their college-age youth. He was told that although he had done a good job in some areas, they had decided he was not suited for the church. He was given a forty-five-day notice and told that his services would no longer be required after that time. There is no question but that he would have profited greatly from periodic evaluation rather than a final judgment that came down like a bombshell upon him.

This is not to say that, at times, firing a staff member is not only appropriate but necessary. Fred Smith, a management consultant in Dallas, once said that if one treats irresponsibility irresponsibly, then one must remember that two wrongs do not make a right. The experience of the minister to singles described above, however, was irresponsible action on the part of senior clergy. They did not know how to supervise and evaluate on a regular basis, and they covered this leadership deficiency by an impulsive firing that resembled surgery rather than treatment!

Someone might ask, Didn't the minister to singles have some responsibility to ask for a performance review? The answer is, Of course. Feedback is just as much the responsibility of subordinates as it is of superiors. Contrary to the old saying, no news is *not* good news. The singles' minister should not have assumed things

were going well. He should have asked for a review of his performance long before he was fired. Len Kageler, a youth pastor in
Seattle, wrote about overcoming his fear of criticism and asking for
feedback:

> I was devastated. I had asked a member in my volunteer youth staff
> to suggest any improvements I needed to make in the ministry. . . ."I'm
> glad you asked, . . ." he began. I knew it was going to be a long lunch.
>
> He explained, in exquisite detail, my deficiencies in handling the
> youth staff. My main problem, as he saw it, was communication. I
> repeatedly failed to give adequate direction. I also failed to help him see
> his role as important. . . .
>
> As I reflected later, other incidents came to mind that corroborated
> what he had said. Just a month earlier, a young couple resigned from
> the team, saying that they didn't feel they knew enough about what
> was going on to be of any help. . . .

After this Kageler began taking people to lunch and asking
dangerous questions.

> Five years have now passed since that staff volunteer leveled with
> me, and since then our church has decided to make feedback a regular
> part of its ministry to us. Despite some of my initial fears, the
> experience has been healthy. I'm thankful for the serious approach. I
> feel both secure and cared for. I know God uses those to whom I am
> accountable to keep me growing and improving. They are my early
> warning system.[10]

Yes, it is the responsibility of staff to ask for regular, periodic
performance reviews. It is the responsibility of the pastor and the
church to give them.

The final characteristic of evaluation with support is that the
staff evaluation procedure should be clearly communicated to the
members of the parish. There should be explicit ways in which
people in the church may voice their commendations and their
recommendations. When these procedures are made public,
behind-the-scenes gossip will be greatly reduced and informal
evaluations curtailed. Furthermore, when these clearly stated
channels and procedures are communicated to the church, parishioners will feel a sense of dignity because of inclusion in the process. At the same time, they will feel assured that there is a plan for
evaluating as well as affirming the staff.

Relationship without Socializing

The final characteristic that will enhance the cohesion and

effectiveness of church staff members is "relationship without socializing." It should go without saying that staff have relationships with each other. The very structure of an organization places workers in a relationship of division of labor, responsibility, authority, and communication. Staff must relate. They cannot avoid it.

It is the quality, rather than the fact, of the relationship that is important to consider. Among church staff members, the quality of the relationship is often idealized and/or confused. A real need exists to define the relationship clearly and abide by that definition scrupulously. When such clear, realistic, nonidealistic, yet spiritual definitions exist, staff cohesion and effectiveness can be expected to increase.

The major difficulty in staff relationships is that the expectations *are* idealistic rather than realistic. In religious institutions, such as the church, such idealism is understandable. Mitchell suggests that staff relationships are models of the church for laypersons.[11] Parishioners look to their ministers to be examples of how Christians ought to relate to each other in the church. Taking their cues from the New Testament admonition that Christians should love one another and from the current emphasis on *koinonia* and fellowship, laypersons as well as clergy have high expectations that relationships will be different in church than in nonreligious organizations.

There is one sense in which these idealistic expectations are, at the same time, realistic. It is realistic to expect church staff members to respect each others' feelings. When differences arise, whether theological, programmatic, stylistic, or procedural, individuals should solve their problems in an honest, yet forgiving, manner.

It is also realistic to expect church staff members to share their faith with each other and to make their service of ministry an offering to God. This means parishioners expect them to be spiritual people by participating in prayer as well as studying theology and the Bible together.

Furthermore, it is realistic to expect church staff to be sensitive to unique stages of life and differing circumstances in life that may exist from time to time. They should never allow the work of the church to blind them to the stress that individual staff members may be undergoing.

However, it is not realistic to expect the church staff experience to be a substitute for family relationships. Nor is it realistic to expect church staff to socialize with each other. In the case of family, these relationships require a quality of unselfish acceptance that is unrealistic for those who work together. To think that clergy should act like family is inappropriately idealistic.

In the case of socializing, it is impossible for those who work in different power relationships to shift perspective and relate as equals on any continuing basis. Although clergy may idealistically hope they can be close friends with each other as well as co-workers, socializing involves them in a dual-role relationship. This usually compromises their ability to function well with each other. Senior pastors find it hard to honestly evaluate junior staff with whom they have related socially. Junior staff members sometimes expect evaluations on the basis of personal attraction rather than job performance if they have become too socially friendly with their senior ministers. Social relationships involve people in a conflict of interest if they also work together. Church staff should have their social relationships outside of their work associations. Parishioners should understand that staff do this because of the realistic danger that doing otherwise handicaps their functioning.

This does not mean that clergy will avoid attending social events together. It does mean, however, that recreational relationships should not be the same as work relationships.

Clergy will have genuine and warm concerns about each others' families. But they should not expect their families to be each others' confidants or best friends. In our judgment, relationship without socializing is an important maxim that characterizes staff cohesion and effectiveness.

Staff relationships are probably the most important aspect of clergy life. In our teaching, we have heard more complaints and received more requests for help regarding clergy staff than about any other aspect of ordained ministry. In this chapter, we have discussed several unique features of clergy motivation and psycho-dynamics. We suggested three characteristics of good staff relation-ships: responsibility with freedom, evaluation with support, and relationship without socializing. Where these characteristics exist, cohesion and effectiveness will occur.

Chapter 10.
Ministerial Effectiveness

It is one thing to be a successful banker. It may be quite another to succeed as a clergyperson. As the old saying goes, ministry is not one of those professions that "pays wages on Saturday." The effect of good ministry may not be known for years. Even more important, being successful as a minister may be something other than the size of the church budget or the number of new members who have joined in the past year. Consider the following examples.

Ignacio, a sixty-three-year-old Episcopal priest, recently underwent surgery for cancer. Even though he undergoes chemotherapy treatments every week, he is still able to lead morning prayer and celebrate the eucharist each Sunday. He can do little else. Ignacio has served in this parish eight years and has a history of thirty-six years in the priesthood. In spite of the fact that the past year has been a loss, he has a record of proven performance—if only in longevity!

Some members of the vestry think their parish priest should take early retirement. During this last year, he has been ill more weeks than he has been healthy, and they have concluded that the parish needs a younger, more vigorous priest. It is easy to see things from their viewpoint. But Ignacio is not ready to retire. He hopes he can talk them into reconsidering.

Sitting in his study, he thinks about the past and the future. His salary has never been high; the present salary is the most money he has ever earned, yet the parish is still a mission church partially supported by the diocese. "Have I been a success?" he wonders, "Does the vestry's request that I retire mean that I am a failure?" He thinks back over the last several years and to the other eight parishes he has served. Thoughts about weddings, baptisms, funerals, eucharists, special programs—all float through his mind. He is unsure.

On the other hand, consider Harold, a United Methodist minister in good health who is fifteen years younger than Ignacio. The Pastor/Parish Relations Committee has requested the bishop to return him to his present church for another year of service.

Harold has moved up the clergy ranks rather quickly. His father served as a pastor in the same area, and Harold has lived in the northwest part of Minnesota all his life. The family name is well known throughout the denomination.

Some ministers have suggested that Harold's family name has influenced his career. He enjoys a wide reputation, however, as one of the very best preachers in the region. Four years ago, the bishop appointed Harold to the largest church in the Annual Conference, and no other church to which he could now move would have as many members, offer as much salary, or have as much prestige as the one in which he currently ministers.

As the meeting of the Annual Conference approached, Harold reminisced with his wife one morning after breakfast about the various churches he had pastored. "Remember those times when we looked forward to the meeting of the Annual Conference because we thought the bishop would appoint us to a larger church?" he asked. "And remember when we hated to leave one church but were eager to move to another? Well, this year," he added, "I'm feeling bored. Where else can we go? I wonder if all those moves to new churches mean that I've been successful or not?"

Obviously, Ignacio and Harold are experiencing two different types of predicament. Each wonders, however, if he has been successful. In a sense, they illustrate two definitions of success with which most clergy would probably disagree: (1) success means longevity and (2) success means bigness.

"Success" Equals Number of Years in Ministry

The first erroneous definition of success is longevity (i.e., the number of years a pastor has ministered in a church). Ignacio has been a priest for thirty-six years. Persistence cannot be considered synonymous with success because, unfortunately, ministry is one of those professions having a high tolerance for mediocrity. Until recently, it has been possible for a minister to move from one church to another throughout his or her lifetime without being significantly effective, simply because the need for clergy outstripped the supply.

Lest we be too harsh on longevity, however, we should note that persistence has some values in such a profession as ministry. After all, leading a voluntary organization such as a church is no easy task, as any experienced minister will attest. Ministry is a high burnout profession, and to continue leading a parish after twenty to thirty years is no small accomplishment.

The most widely used measurement of vocational interest, the Strong Campbell Interest Inventory, uses length of years in ministry as its major criterion for choosing a group of successful ministers against whom to compare candidates. But it uses only three years as an index of persistence! Ministers like Ignacio and Harold far outstrip this figure. If being in ministry for three years is considered noteworthy, then twenty to thirty years should be considered amazing!

Longevity may be even more significant at this time in history when the supply of ordained clergy is greater than the demand and where the "call" system of ministerial selection is becoming more and more common. Even United Methodist bishops find it increasingly difficult to say by fiat which minister will and will not be assigned to a given church.

The number of years in a particular pastorate may be a less questionable and a more positive standard of success in ministry than we have presumed. Longevity has two sides. On the one hand, it may be a valid measure of effectiveness, while on the other hand, it may be a sign of mediocrity.

"Success" Means Bigness

The second definition of success with which most clergy would disagree is that success means bigness—either in terms of size of membership or size of salary. If bigness meant success, Harold would be successful while Ignacio would not. Although Harold is pleased to be the pastor of a large church, we do not believe he would think that the size of a pastor's church should be the sole criterion for assessing ministerial success.

Bigness may be a peculiarly Western idea of success. Inclusion in the "Fortune 500" list would probably be an undisputed goal for every business in the Western world. The commercial world takes it for granted that "bigger means better." Religion may have been seduced by this maxim. Studies of churches that have gained the most members and have the largest budgets have featured regularly in the pages of many clergy journals.[1] It has been presumed that ministers who led such churches were the most successful even though many thoughtful critics have suggested ministry should be judged by other criteria.

Well over 75 percent of the churches in America have less than 150 members, and many of these churches pay their pastors minimal salaries. Ignacio served such parishes. Would all these ministers be considered unsuccessful purely on the basis of membership size and minister's salary? We think not. Such a judgment would condemn the majority of clergy to failure. The church might better remember that it has one foot in heaven and one on earth, as Augustine suggested. Furthermore, God calls the church to be faithful, rather than successful as the world views success.

Perhaps faithfulness is dependent, in an absolute sense, on whether the Word is preached and the sacraments are administered, as Martin Luther concluded. In a world where the good news is always the hard news, there ordinances may be the only legitimate criteria worthy of note and the only valid signs of success. If this is true, bigness may be evidence of bad faith if it means that the message of the gospel has been diluted or neglected.

Bigness may be similar to longevity. There may be another side to bigness. In a provocative book entitled *And Are We Yet Alive?* Richard Wilke noted that 60 percent of the churches in his denomination had no confirmation class and that 66 percent of the churches had baptized four or fewer persons during the last year.[2] When compared to the fact that by far the great majority of new Christians become members of larger churches, these are sobering statistics. If these figures are representative of all denominations, the success of churches in an evangelistic religion such as Christianity may, indeed, be related to bigness.

Perhaps there is a sense in which the ability of a church to gain and hold members is directly related to the leadership of the minister. A study of growing Churches of Christ in Orange County, California, supported this conclusion.[3] In no small measure, becoming a pastor in the larger churches may be an indication of success. Certainly, the current emphasis on training clergy in church growth principles could be considered an effort to make ministers more effective. In a study of effective Missouri Synod Lutheran pastors, Nauss found that they were more frequently located in larger churches, about which he wrote, "These characteristics would be the results expected of an effective ministry."[4] There may be some truth to Nauss' conclusion.

Nevertheless, longevity and bigness may need to be combined with or incorporated into other criteria, rather than considered separately, as indices of successful ministry. A more inclusive model for clergy success or effectiveness is needed. Such a model will now be discussed.

A Model for Clergy Effectiveness

The first step in constructing a model of this type is to describe how success and effectiveness relate to each other. Although we have used these terms somewhat synonymously, there is a need to make their relationship clear.

For ministers to be successful, they must be *effective*. Success means "having an effect" or "being influential." Having an effect on what? Being influential in what ways? Answering these questions requires reconsideration of the nature of ministry itself.

Without the church, there are no clergy. Being a clergyperson in the Christian tradition means serving as a minister or priest of the church. Therefore, being successful or effective means having influence in, and effect upon, the church. Thus, it is quite appropriate to note longevity of ministry and size of membership when determining effectiveness. These factors alone, however, do not indicate what the church attempts to do and what kind of effect it endeavors to have on its members and in the larger society in an ongoing way.

Theologically, the Christian church is a means of grace (i.e., it is the God-appointed agent of reconciliation in the world). For clergy to be successful or have effect, they must do so in terms of this mission of the church. Therefore, they should be evaluated in terms of whether they have been influential in reconciling people to God through the ministrations of the church.

With this in mind, we suggest the following model. It makes a distinction between primary, secondary, and tertiary dimensions of clergy effect on the church as ways in which people are reconciled to God by grace through faith.[5]

Primary criteria for clergy effectiveness pertain to changes in people's insights and understandings. Secondary criteria pertain to changes in people's attitudes. Tertiary criteria pertain to changes in people's behaviors that result from these changes in their insights and attitudes.

Primary Criteria: Changes in Insights and Understandings

Primarily, ministry is intended to have effect on people. Initially, then, clergy can be judged on whether they have been influential in changing the inner experience of individuals in terms of their insights or understandings about the nature of life and the love of God. Insights are those novel and revolutionary perceptions occurring in people as a result of their response to the gospel message. They are inner reformations of personal identity that come through conversions and deepening insights at critical moments of worship, study, and religious experience at which ministers are present.

In a sense, this is the "new birth" about which Jesus spoke to Nicodemus (see John 3:1ff) and the experience about which the farmer spoke in William James' classic *The Varieties of Religious Experience*. The farmer stated that after his conversion everything looked new, even the horses, pigs, and chickens! Although various traditions might determine the method and interpret the results of these experiences in different ways, the centrality of this transformation in self-perception cannot be denied.

Understandings follow insights. Whereas insights have to do with personal identity and basic outlook, understandings pertain to reinterpretations that result from seeing life events through the eyes of faith. These reconsiderations of situations and episodes, of joys and tragedies, of moments and years, of growth and development, and of stability and change come through as an individual experiences a sense of God's presence and providence in daily life.

These new understandings result from a developmental deepening guided by the ministries of clergy in their pastoral role. One could state that insights imply a "state of mind" while understandings imply a "trait of outlook." Traits are characteristic modes of behavior. Ideally, the trait of Christian understanding involves the ability to perceive transcendent meaning in all the events of life. This would include perceiving God's presence in good times and bad, as well as the inclination to hear the call of God to justice and faithful service.

In the past several years, we have attempted to develop a structured interview for measuring the extent to which people have achieved these Christian insights and understandings.[6] We have labeled this *religious maturity*. Extensive research has convinced us that those for whom their faith works, or is "mature," are the ones capable of living courageously and victoriously. We have found that those judged in our interviews as more mature are likely to be less anxious, less depressed, and higher in self-esteem.[7] Older women, rated as more religiously mature, were inclined to experience less depression and disillusionment irrespective of how much tragedy they had experienced.[8] As yet, we have not compared the average maturity level of parishioners of clergy rated more or less successful, but our conviction is that there would be significant differences among them.

Taken together, insights and understandings are the basic dimensions on which clergy effect should be judged. Other effects stem from these basic inner changes. Although these effects are difficult to measure, they can be inferred, in part, from the secondary and tertiary dimensions (i.e., attitudes and behaviors).

But just because people enjoy coming to church (the secondary attitudinal criterion) or attend and give their money (the tertiary behavioral criterion) does not necessarily mean that their inner insights and attitudes have changed. These attitudes and behaviors can be indications of family expectations, habits, and cultural conformity. It is still essential to find ways of assessing whether ministers have truly had any effects on changes in basic insights and understandings of their parishioners. Perhaps our approach, labeled the Religious Status Interview, will prove to be a viable method for assessing these vital processes.[9]

Secondary Criteria: Changes in Attitudes

The secondary criteria for effectiveness pertain to attitudes that change as a result of clergy influence. Attitudes are inner predispositions to respond in certain ways to various events. They are not the responses themselves. Attitudes have to do with feelings about, evaluations of, and inner reactions to church activities and religious teachings and ideals. For example, if people wake up on Sunday morning and want to go to the morning service or to a church school class, it could be said that they have a positive attitude. If, when people are tempted to cheat others or to violate their morals, they experience guilt and resist those inclinations, it could be said that they have a positive attitude toward religious ideals.

These verbal and thoughtful expressions of satisfaction/approval or dissatisfaction/disapproval determine the degree of motivation that people have for supporting or participating in the life of the church. It is here that the way clergy perform their duties becomes crucial. Their style and behavior almost always become the focus around which these attitudes develop. For good or ill, clergy become the focus of people's likes or dislikes about the church and religion. Research suggests that people no longer tend to choose churches on the basis of tradition or denomination. Rather, they shop around and go where they like the minister and where they have friends. This makes clergy exist much more in a market-place than they ever thought possible.

People can evidence positive attitudes toward ministers' preaching, leading, administering, and worship celebration without having attendant inner changes in insights or understandings. For example, an individual might report that she or he liked a pastor's personality and the liveliness of the worship service without this statement implying any inner insight or understanding about the true nature of the Christian life.

The reverse can also be true. Inner changes can occur in parishioners even when they do not approve of certain ministerial styles or personalities or methods. Those who have come to know themselves as saved by God's grace through faith might have a dislike for a minister in a given church. It should be noted, however, that in modern America, this is becoming more and more rare. Unfortunately, positive attitudes seem to exist and persist much more commonly where people respond approvingly to clergy than where they do not.

In the ideal situation, and increasingly in the typical situation, inner changes in insights and understanding, noted as primary criteria, are followed by the attitudinal changes that are considered secondary criteria. The more effective clergypersons are, the more these results will follow from their ministries. This means that clergy should be judged on whether people like to participate in church services that they lead and the activities that they sponsor. This should not blind clergy, however, to the possibilities that these preferences or approvals do not always imply that inner life change has occurred.

This means that clergy should regularly and constantly check and note how people feel about the life of the church. It is not enough to listen to what people say in the reception line at the back of the church after morning worship service. This may make the priest/pastor feel good, but it is not a good indication of people's attitudes. There are many more creative and systematic ways of gaining feedback about how people feel about the clergy, the church, and the activities it sponsors. Church members often feel they are not asked and have no power. This leads to undercover gossip and withdrawal of interest. Often the basic changes in insights and understandings, which prompted church attendance in the first place, are reduced to cynicism and disillusionment because of changes in attitudes. Secondary changes in attitudes are indeed important measures of clergy success.

Tertiary Criteria: Changes in Behavior

Tertiary criteria are the common ones to which people refer when considering whether clergy are effective or not. These are the obvious behaviors—the kinds of events that everyone who is present can see. Size of church and number of people attending worship are often used to measure clergy success, as noted earlier.

Another measure sometimes observed is the amount of average monetary offering or the size of the church budget.

Such criteria are behaviors exhibited by people in response to the gospel as mediated by the church under the leadership of the clergy. The degree to which people take an active part in and give time and money to the church is an index of their involvement and perception that the church meets their needs. These are the outer indices of clergy effect. Since people vote with their presence and their money, a typical method of assessing success considers the attendance and budget. Who participates and who gives are behaviors that can readily be seen and measured. Ideally, they result from insights, understandings, and attitudes—the first two measures of effectiveness discussed earlier.

Retailers certainly look at the results of advertising in this way. By advertising, they attempt to awaken a need for their product (i.e., change the self-perception of the buyer). They then hope to motivate the person toward their product (i.e., change attitudes). Finally, their intent is that the individual will come into the store and buy the product (i.e., they want to influence actual behavior).

These same ideas underlie this three-step model of ministerial effectiveness. The church is very similar to commercial organizations in the way it functions.[10] It has a product to "sell" (i.e., the grace of Almighty God). After presuming that people have an essential need for this product, it attempts to package the product in a way that awakens the need and evokes interest. The "attractiveness" of the church's product is directly related to the performance of its ministers. Although this may seem like a crude comparison to some readers, it is a realistic appraisal of how the church functions in the modern world.

As with the secondary criteria, however, the behaviors of participation and giving do not always mean inner change. People can attend church and put money in the offering without having their insights and understandings changed by the Christian message. This is at the same time regrettable and sad. Religion in our society is culturally acceptable; it is even culturally expected. The motivations behind religious activity may not always be those implied in criteria one and two.

People can be religiously active for very different reasons. Much work in the past twenty years has focused on the distinction between "intrinsic" and "extrinsic" motivations for being religious. This distinction, originally suggested by the well-known psychologist Gordon Allport, differentiates those who come to church in order to socialize and make friends, as well as business contacts, from those who attend church to worship God and fulfill their individual needs for a transcendent dimension in life.[11]

While attending church activities and giving money for religious causes not always indicate inner change, the reverse can also be true. We think it is theologically correct to say that the Christian faith *is* the Christian church. Being "religious" in a Christian sense means active involvement in the church.

Christian faith is rooted in the Jewish faith, which, in turn, is grounded in the doctrine of election. The call of Abraham, the choice of the Hebrews to be a holy nation, the Davidic monarchy, the synagogue of the Diaspora, the remnant teachings of the eighth-century prophets, the revelation of God in Jesus, and the establishment of the New Testament church are all essential ingredients of Christian faith. The Christian religion is not individual but corporate.

Christianity probably differs most radically from the other religions of the world in having this quality of corporateness. The inner changes and the positive attitudes that result from effective ministry should result in overt church-related behavior. Individual Christianity is not Christianity. Individuals may well be religious, but they are not mature Christians unless they are members of the church. Nevertheless, it is likely correct that in God's economy, the church is a means to the end, not the end in itself. Thus the church, as well as the clergy, may eventually be expendable! Yet on this side of heaven, the church is essential, and this third criterion for assessing clergy success is definitely church related.

This model of primary, secondary, and tertiary criteria for effectiveness provides a useful tool for understanding how ministers view success. Obviously, these criteria exist along a continuum of "soft" to "hard" data. Insights, understandings, and attitudes are soft data; they are difficult to measure and may change from time to time. They exist inside the person and are available only through listening to what people say about themselves. Hard data are the behaviors that others can see (i.e., attendance and giving).

This brings up certain questions: Can people be trusted? Do they really know the truth about themselves? Have they truly come to a new awareness of themselves and the world, and was this transformation due to the ministry of the clergy? These crucial questions cannot be ignored and may be more important measures of effectiveness than the hard data of the number of church services attended and the amount of dollars contributed—regardless of what one has concluded about the importance of overt church behavior.

As Burley Howe, a researcher in this field, suggests, one must define effectiveness in terms of "having effect on those ministered to."[12] He concludes that we need to be clear about what clergy hope to achieve in people's lives. Liking the way a minister performs tasks, agreeing with the content of sermons, participating in church activities, and even giving many dollars to church causes may be interesting and important. But one must still ask the question, Are these the primary indices of effect by which ministers should be judged?

We think not. The primary effects of changed insights and understandings must still be considered primary. Although difficult to measure, they should not be ignored. Howe uses the example of physicians in private practice. He concludes that the only appropriate measure of physicians' success is whether their patients get well, not the size of their practices, the elegance of their offices, their bedside manners, or their sophisticated knowledge about medical literature. These activities are instrumental means to an end but not the primary goal. Likewise with ministers. Task performance and personal attractiveness are means to an end: the changed identity and altered life-perception of people resulting from changes in insights and understandings.

Clergy as Enablers

Howe adds one further dimension to this issue that we would like to emphasize. He pictures clergy as *enablers*. This term for ministers ties together the soft and hard data of the three criteria discussed above. It enriches the picture of participation and giving in a way that integrally relates them to the inner changes of identity and motivation that we consider primary indices of effect.

An enabler is one who empowers, provides ways, and makes it possible for something to happen. In the case of ministry, to enable people means to provide ways and resources whereby they can act on the new self-insight, understanding, and motivation gained from receiving the Christian gospel. This is where the church as a means of grace comes in. Not only do people hear a transforming message that changes their identity through the ministry of the church, but the church becomes the channel through which they can express these new perceptions. Where the church is effective, people feel they have found a way to live out their faith. Where the church is ineffective, people feel inhibited and constrained by what the church offers. Effective or successful ministry enables individuals to express their motivation to be Christian in meaningful ways that fulfill their new self-understanding. In his provocative book *The Church in the Way*, James Dittes concludes that, whereas many have felt the institutional church gets "in the way" of the gospel, the church, in fact, is the means by which people can find a way of acting on their faith. According to Dittes the church is essential, not optional.[13] And church administration is a critical means to effective ministry.

In this sense, clergy as enablers are like a coach and an athletic director all in one. The athletic director plans the schedule, provides the equipment, and prepares the playing field. The coach then guides the players and directs the game. Minister-enablers do these things. In the church setting, they provide meaningful activities and opportunities for people to express their faith. They also work with individuals by counseling and guiding them in a manner that helps each individual find fulfilling places of service for God.

This enabling role could be called "developmental ministry."[14] Developmental ministers see their primary role as that of enabling people to find fulfillment through the life of the church. Because of this, developmental clergy are interested in the third kind of criteria noted above (i.e., whether people come to church activities and whether they give money to the church).

Individuals, however, are always the prime concern of developmental clergy; they are more interested in people than in programs. These ministers resist judging their success on the basis of how many attend a given program or whether the offering is large or small. They find ways of talking with their church members in order to learn if these parishioners regularly find fulfillment in what the church offers. They consistently express interest in helping people find a ministry that provides personal satisfaction. And to keep this satisfaction from becoming stagnant, they endeavor to broaden the vision of their parishioners.

We began this chapter with vignettes about Ignacio and Harold, two ministers who questioned their success in ministry. We noted that while length of years of service and size of church membership are possible measures of success, they are insufficient by themselves. A proposed three-step model involving changes in (1) insights and understandings, (2) attitudes, and (3) behaviors poses some limitations but significant possibilities as an approach for measuring success. The prime role of a minister is to be an enabler because success in ministry is based primarily on the effect clergy have on those to whom they minister.

Chapter 11.
The Life Cycle of Ministry

The cool, damp earth of his postage-stamp-size garden was a welcome contrast to the warm spring sun. The Reverend Ebenezer Martin covered the last pod of squash seeds and reached for the package of bean seeds to plant along the cyclone fence. He paused and reminisced about this springtime ritual of several years. The cycle seems so profoundly simple, he thought: first the seed, then the young plant, then the blooms that promise results, then the battle with the insects and the hot, dry summer to bring as much as possible to harvest. Finally would come the withering of the mature plants as they ended their cycle of productivity—leaving behind their seed for the next season.

"So profound, so utterly biblical," mused Ebenezer. "Just like my work as a pastor. Like St. Paul said, 'I planted, Apollos watered, and God gives the increase.' I can see this cycle in my work with Mount Zion Church. I came as their rector like a seed to be planted. Together we have produced much. At some point, it will be time to move on to another parish."

Ebenezer began placing the beans in the row and covering them. "I suppose my whole life as a pastor is something like this basic cycle. College and seminary were the initial seeds for my career. Then I planted myself at Calvary Chapel. That success led to more fruit at the Church of the Resurrection. Now I'm beginning to see signs of slowing down. God, I hope I'm not withering on the vine! Yet it is inevitable that at some point I will end my career as a pastor. I guess I'll attend that seminar on preparing for retirement. But in the meantime, I have work to do in this parish." He reached for the garden hose to give this year's crop its first drink of water.

Wheels within Wheels—Cycles within Cycles

The concept of life cycle is now a solid cornerstone of all adult development theoretical frameworks. Since chronological age is easiest to measure objectively, terms such as *young adult*, *adult*, and *senior citizen* have become widely recognized and used. Our society attributes many kinds of changes to age, although it is more the meaning of a given age rather than the age itself that is the key to life cycle. To turn age thirty, be over the hill at age forty, or be eligible for retirement benefits at age sixty-two or sixty-five are only a few of our life cycle markers.

A cycle suggests two poles of a unitary process: differentiation and assimilation. Both of these emerge from the wellsprings of life nurturing set in a time perspective. This cycle could also be called liberating and conserving, separation and integration, change and continuity, or moving outward and moving inward. Theologically, we may also think of this process as creating and redeeming, set in the context of the sustaining nurture of the Holy Spirit.

The ministerial life cycle is an example of a vocational life cycle. We can apply the five common elements in the vocational development process to the minister:

1. *Preparation:* college and seminary
2. *Entry Level:* usually the first three to five years after ordination
3. *Advancement:* the next five to twenty years when "promotions" most often occur as one moves from a smaller to a larger parish
4. *Maintenance:* the zenith period from the last major advancement to the first steps toward retirement
5. *Decline:* from the initial reductions of responsibilities to complete retirement; some prefer to call this step "retirement/reengagement."

If we apply this cycle to one's full adult vocational life—from approximately age eighteen through the sixties or seventies, a span of forty to fifty years—these periods would coincide approximately with the following ages:

1. *Preparation:* early twenties
2. *Entry Level:* latter twenties through early thirties
3. *Advancement:* thirties through forties; sometimes fifties
4. *Maintenance:* late forties through early sixties
5. *Decline:* late fifties through sixties; perhaps seventies.

If one already has had a career in another field, however, she or he would have left that career at one of the five points above and become involved in resolving that career stage with one of the career stages of ministry. For example, if an individual had retired from government or military service after twenty years, he or she might begin preparation for ministry around age forty or forty-five. The entry level period may then be shortened, partly due to one's age and previous life experience, as well as opportunities. (Sometimes, it seems, all congregations assume that all ministers are between the ages of thirty-five and forty-five!) The other stages would also be affected in similar ways.

This framework is not a smooth trajectory like the path of a long football pass or home run. Rather, many ups and downs represent additional shorter-range cycles within the life cycle. One's vocational cycles also interact with many other cycles. Among these are one's family and personal cycles of events; the life cycles of relatives, friends, and work associates; cycles of one's parishioners and people in the community; the cycles of growth or decline of local churches and communities; and local, national, and world events.

Taken together from the perspective of the individual clergyperson, perhaps these interacting cycles are more like the fireworks of New Year's Day or Independence Day celebrations. The individual rockets have their own cycle within the ordered sequence of the show.

Critical Times in the Life Cycle

Any time of change is potentially a critical time in the ministerial life cycle. Change produces stress, but stress in itself is neither hurtful nor helpful. Rather, it is the ratio of the coping resources of the individual to the amount of perceived stress (both in awareness and outside of conscious awareness) that determines whether a change will be beneficial or detrimental.

Individual coping power is composed of skills that are guided by intentions and activated by energy. The following points in the life cycle may or may not be critical for an individual personally. Whether they are or are not depends upon the correlation between the stress one perceives in the event and the coping power one brings to the event.

A 1984 study of seminarians found that those who perceived change as a challenge and opportunity rather than as an obstacle or danger had lower situational anxiety scores and higher grade point averages.[1] Whether change is a challenge or a danger is related to the confidence individuals have in their strength for coping with those changes. Because they have greater personal and professional resources, it is likely that the more competent ministers are less threatened by changes. Again, however, this is moderated by the expectations of the individual. A minister who feels trapped or threatened may turn the occasion into an opportunity to minister.[2]

Based on the work of several researchers, some typical critical life cycle times, with brief attention to the reasons, can be identified.[3]

1. Graduation from seminary involves a change from an academic setting to the real world in which application and competence must be demonstrated daily among real dilemmas with people.

2. The three to five years after seminary or ordination are typically a time to evaluate the one or more parish moves that may have occurred (asking whether these are "promotions") and to refine career directions in the context of actual experience. Family factors (such as ages of children) and personal factors (such as the symbolic meaning of turning age thirty or forty) may also be involved.

3. Around age forty, when important goals have not been reached, occurs another reassessment of career rewards vs. career goals. For some, the initial impact of a family "empty nest" (perhaps welcomed or dreaded) and one's own death in a more specific number of years may also begin to surface.

4. Retirement may be anticipated as a time of insecurity. Dependency and financial factors may be part of anticipating retirement. Some may see no other way to be active than in the ministry. Health problems may also increase prior to retirement.

5. A move to a new parish means leaving good friends and familiar social networks and entering—perhaps unknowingly—potential conflict situations in the new parish.

6. Conflict between pastor and congregation may raise questions of one's character, integrity, honesty, and competence. Competition and hidden agendas may emerge. Unresolved personal issues with one's family of origin or current family may surface.

7. Changes in denomination structures, such as having a new superior (superintendent, bishop, etc.) usually changes the

power structure in a judicatory. Depending on how much control these structures have over the local parish, a change will probably force a minister to redevelop power relations with the new superior and people he or she places in leadership positions.

Elements in the Life Cycle

The ministerial life cycle is an ecological system only partly controlled by physical aging. While biological changes form an essential part of the picture, research shows several major factors that affect the ministerial life cycle. We can class these variables into two clusters: intrapsychic and environmental.

Intrapsychic Variables

The cluster of intrapsychic variables are individual factors that we can, to some degree, control and/or modify.

Expectations

In a study of 341 clergy from thirty-six denominations and forty-three states, William Moore showed that unrealistic expectations are a major factor in burnout of pastors.[4] One's expectations as an individual and as a pastor have many roots.

Expectations begin in one's family of origin, as suggested by Friedman.[5] The support from family and friends for one's decision and continuation in professional ministry is often a positive motivational factor.[6]

As children, however, some ministers were placed in a type of "little adult" role in their family of origin. Becoming a minister may have been motivated partly by a desire to please mother and/or father and, by implication, God. To the extent that this happens, the individual will be unable to relax from these excessive expectations because current accomplishments cannot satisfy the internalized "mom and dad" voices from childhood. The individual never feels "good enough" or sufficiently successful. When these expectations are projected as coming from God, their weight is infinite and often ends in the despair of never being able to satisfy what one perceives as "requirements."

The answer to this dilemma of excessive expectations upon oneself is to recognize the grace of God's unconditional love for us. This is easier said than done. Sometimes an individual grows to this realization through personal prayer, devotions, or a program of

intentional spiritual formation. Often, however, it requires sufficient time with an appropriate mentor or therapist to trace the
many connections between expectations and unresolved dimensions of one's childhood family.

The other major source of expectations is in current events and
relationships. When an individual accepts her or his strengths and
limitations as a finite being, the expectations for success in
ministry and as a person are realistic, flexible, and achievable. An
individual may experience this in the acceptance and support of
spouse, family, friends, and colleagues. Because of the grace of
their love, the individual is free to decide which tasks and roles he
or she can best seek and accomplish.

Competencies

As Jesus noted in the parable of the talents, individuals have
various combinations of abilities. Some ministers appear to have
the attractive appearance, the facility with words, the ability to
remember names, and the gift of golden tongue to draw supporters (even if emotionally dependent) and are seemingly in-
stantly accepted anywhere. Since success in ministry is so often, if
superficially, judged on these and other highly visible characteristics, people who bring these qualities to their work as a pastor
have a running start on success.

At more substantive levels, individuals with keener memories,
capacity for more complex cognitive functioning, and other
leadership and social skills, which are needed by a congregation in
their pastoral leader, are more likely to be called or assigned to the
better churches. Although opportunity may knock, only those who
have the competencies requested will be able to open the door.

The fields may be ready for harvest, but having enough competent laborers to do the job is the challenge. As our civilization
becomes increasingly complex, the demand for pastors with higher
levels of competence in more areas will also increase. Since
competition at the top is keener and decided much more precisely,
the direction of one's lifetime ministry journey is, and will continue
to be, heavily affected by the degree to which one's competence is
superior to others who are available.

Obviously, some pastors are more competent than others. In
charting one's ministerial life cycle, competence is a major factor.
Feeling confident and accepted by God—when one admits, after
honest preparation and self-inventory, that a lower level of lifetime
success and earnings will be okay—is indeed a key acceptance of
God's grace.

Interests

Vocational interests guide one's ministerial career because they underlie one's choices about spending time and energy. Across one's ministerial life cycle, an individual may modify the priority given to various roles. As solo pastor of one (or more) congregations at entry levels, a minister may be his or her own "specialist" in all areas needed for ministry. Working as an associate on a church staff, however, may lead to specializing in specific areas such as age-level ministries, administration, social witness, mission outreach, counseling, or parish visitation.

Interests may change according to one's experience in a particular type of ministry. Some prefer the excitement of new information and challenges and, therefore, become bored and tired doing the same kinds of work each year. Others enjoy the security and comfort of becoming increasingly proficient in doing the same types of work for many years.

The key is successfully matching one's interests and the requirements of a particular pastorate or other setting. Vocational assessment and counseling can assist a minister at any stage to examine her or his own interests in relation to requirements for ministry. The Myers-Briggs Type Inventory mentioned in chapter 2, and the Inventory of Religious Activities and Interests and the Theological School Inventory described in chapter 3 are all helpful in this regard. Sometimes loss of interest may be symptomatic of deeper personal conflicts that produce depression and loss of energy. Interest shifts may also be a sign of experiences in evaluation or in perceived competence in a given area of ministry.

Commitment

Commitment is one's basic decision or will to go in a certain direction. Initial commitment to becoming an ordained minister involves both "special leading" and "natural leading" types of calling.[7] Special leading expresses one's sense of transcendental calling in which one responds, through ministry, to God's initiative. This is one's vision that transcends the current times of discouragement and motivates when all other motivations seem lost.

Natural leading is the sense in which one sees evidences of God's calling in the daily activities of one's life. It is perceiving God at work immanently in the part of creation that directly touches one's personal life. It is the feeling that results continue to confirm that one belongs in the ministry, a sense of good fit between what the ministry needs and what one can do.

These two dimensions are not correlated; this means that each contributes in a unique way to an individual's commitment. They tend to interface with each other. If special leading is the "stretch" to fit a new pair of shoes, natural leading is the corresponding sense of "old shoe fit" in the ministry. Commitment is acknowledging both the "new wineskins for new wine" as well as the "old wine in old wineskins."

Commitment changes across one's lifetime. The sense of commitment to follow God's leading completely may at times imply leaving the ordained ministry or changing to a different place in the church structure or staying doggedly in a parish that, to the external observer, may seem to provide few noticeable rewards.

The main components of commitment are subjective feelings of challenge and skill. In a study of 667 ministers in the Chicago area, the most predictive elements of commitment to ministry were a sense of personal fulfillment, spouse's satisfaction with her or his self-chosen roles in the marriage and in the parish, and good staff relationships.[8]

Another study of 215 Protestant clergy showed that commitment shifted across the life span but generally increased with age. Nor was there strong evidence for a "mid-life transition" or period of self-doubt and reevaluation.[9] Ministers in this study placed highest priority on their marriage and family relationships and relatively lower priority on social and civic responsibility. The largest increases in career satisfaction occurred for ministers whose oldest child was age three to six. In common with other studies, ministers whose oldest child was age six to thirteen reported the lowest levels of marriage satisfaction.

These and other studies suggest that one's commitment to ministry is affected by what is happening in one's life in the parish and in one's family. They correspond with the increase in satisfaction that comes from the payoffs of promotions and other recognition of competence, which usually initially appears in the career advancement stage. They also correspond with the sobering feedback as one "levels off" into the maintenance stage, which tends to happen about the time one's children enter the teenage launching stage of family development.

An important implication for ministers: when commitment seems to wane, look for what else is happening in one's life. The "spiritual dryness" periods have been known in spiritual formation efforts for centuries. Used wisely, these periods can be times of deepening commitments in search of the nourishment of God's Spirit. Commitment will go higher and lower across one's lifetime;

do not be surprised when it goes to a low point. Instead, a wise minister, in consultation with other people, will look closely at roots, goals, interests, and competencies as one continues to shape a ministerial career.

Energy

Some ministers have more energy than others, just as some ministers are taller or heavier than others. Energy level is, in part, a genetic characteristic. One may easily observe this while standing outside a hospital nursery and watching the newborns. Several relax and peacefully sleep; others squirm, twist, and cry. People who regularly work with newborns become especially sensitive to the inherent differences among people even at this early age. Parents also note this in their families when they describe one child as noisy, more active, or energetic in comparison with another child. Some families are also much more active, excitable, and dramatic than others.

Each of us has a natural level of activity and available energy that may be affected in many ways. Normal "good" tiredness results from doing useful work, followed by enjoying rest and relaxation as a recharging time for the next cycle of work and rest. All people have biorhythm cycles (although not precisely predictable from birthdate!) across the week, month, and year that affect the level of available energy at any given time.

Unhealthy tiredness and lowered energy may signal anxiety, fear, or hopelessness displayed in clinical depression. The roots of this condition, typically, lie in some combination of current events and past experiences. When energy level is markedly lower than usual, this may signal a need to deal with early burnout signals, an opportunity to retreat for renewal, or perhaps the necessity to consult a therapist about possible hidden factors.

Environmental Variables

The second cluster of elements in the life cycle are the environmental variables. These are factors that influence the ministerial cycle but are beyond our primary control. We may indirectly control them through the individual (intrapsychic) factors listed above.

Opportunities

In any denomination, usually more entry-level parishes (i.e., small churches) exist than large, prestigious churches. By implication, only a few ministers can ever hope to serve in "megachurches." Not enough of these opportunities are available for all the ministers who may have this as part of their lifetime goal. The same can be said for churches that may seem desirable, such as a growing church in a growing suburb. These images are only one definition of opportunity.

By contrast, Jesus reminded us that "the poor we have always." There are many additional "opportunities" to minister that may not seem as socially desirable or easily identifiable. Opportunity, in contrast with crisis or roadblock, is one's own perception of challenge and possibility in a given set of events.

In addition, some highly visible events occur only occasionally or "once in a lifetime." Organizing a new congregation, breaking ground for a new sanctuary, or celebrating paying off a debt are big events set in the context of much underlying hard work. The combination of skills as a "fiery prophet in camel's hair" may be needed only occasionally by a denomination or community. If the wheel has already been invented at a particular time and place, one's skill at inventing wheels is not required there.

Family Factors

The stage of development of one's family also influences the ministerial life cycle. Clergy with elementary-age children probably prefer to locate in a community with good schools, rather than one with schools having major drug problems or inadequate teaching staff. A clergyperson whose teenager expects to graduate from high school next year will have more family pressure not to move this year to a "better church."

If one's spouse has a professional career, a minister may feel much more limited in the number of parishes he or she considers in a move. A minister with an aging, infirm parent may prefer to pastor a church that enables frequent and regular visits with the parent.

These situations illustrate the conflict between expectations in career advancement/advantage and expectations about marriage and family concerns. In the short range, ministers may need to put the needs of other family members ahead of their own career advancement. In the long range, a minister and family can possibly chart potential career decisions according to the impact on each family member.

One way to look at long-range career direction is to consider at which stages in life a minister may be able to serve in a less desirable "hardship" parish. When a judicatory has a policy that every minister serves in such a parish sometime during their ministerial career, the dimensions of these decisions will be different for each minister.

Possible guidelines could be developed. For example, ministers without children (either before children come or after children leave home) would serve in a situation where the supports for children are less. Some would object, saying the minister's family should not be shielded from suffering. Others might note that all ministers, especially the more competent ones, are needed in the difficult parishes even more than in the affluent, more pleasant ones.

Tragedies and Unexpected Events

Although general trends can be predicted rather accurately, few specific events at a specified time and place can be predicted. These unexpected events do affect career directions. They may be personal, as an automobile accident that leaves permanent injury to oneself or family members. Tragedies may happen in the parish, such as the unexpected death of key leaders or a fire or flood that causes major damage to the church building. Events such as a major financial depression or steep inflation may occur in the local, national, or world society.

Among resources for assistance in helping ministers cope at times of unexpected events are the principles for crisis counseling.[10] These include important steps such as (1) identifying the nature of the unexpected event that makes it a crisis, (2) involving one's own and others' resources for coping, and (3) charting short- and long-range goals for a solution.

Results and Rewards

Implicit in the above factors are the results and rewards that come to a minister. The "poor preacher" image or expectation is no longer widespread or viable in today's technical society. While a minister's reported salary may seem lower than most other professional groups, additional advantages of parsonage or house allowance, travel allowance, study leave, and other financial remunerations make some ministers' salaries much higher than the national average for all workers.

In this context, a genuine raise in salary—in contrast with a "token" raise—does impact a minister, just like other workers. Most ministers assume they can serve God equally well in a parish that pays a good salary as one that pays poorly. Ministers' expectations today are higher than in former generations. One study of 125 pastors found that salary accounted for only 11 percent of the variance in their job satisfaction.[11] Another study showed that most clergy were generally satisfied with their salary level.[12]

Rewards have many more subtle effects on life cycle. It is not only the actual salary, number of members received, or other countable items in the inventory of accomplishments but the subjective meanings of these for a pastor that influence one's career directions. One study confirmed findings of several previous studies in showing that ministerial motivation and commitment, which in turn directly affect career directions, increase when the minister feels able to control her or his career directions. Centralization of authority, hierarchical structures, standardization, and formalization of church procedures tend to reduce commitment and set the stage for ministers to be less satisfied in their work. These same factors influence ministers to leave the parish.[13]

Rewards are important. Perhaps clergy are becoming more honest about influences of rewards on their choices and behavior. While some accuse pastors of becoming more secular and worldly, others see this as applying wisdom and insight to a more conscious level of decisions about one's ministerial life career.

God

Oh, yes, we assume that God is involved in each of these factors. But we still need to state that the dimension of the presence and guidance of the Holy Spirit in all areas of life is the underlying basis and the surrounding presence in all of them. Thinking in psychological or business management terms about one's ministerial life cycle does not reduce God's involvement. Far from it. Rather, our appreciation of God's continuing creative and redemptive presence in our current world of activities is increased. Like the scientist whose study of nature shows the details of how God creates, attention to the details of factors that influence one's ministerial career can give an individual conscious awareness of his or her part in the life journey. This reduces the sense of inability, powerlessness, and lack of control. It increases our vision of possibilities and options so that we can more actively influence the directions that we take.

Each minister has a life cycle. Depending upon one's theology and psychology, some will say that the life cycle continues to unfold, implying perhaps more passive personal control and much more external control by others. An alternate systemic view is that one creates one's own ministerial journey out of the material of experiences, opportunities, and choices. Others are involved in the journey, just as we are involved in their journeys.[14]

Ministers combine personal and situational factors to create their ministerial life cycles. Certain times during life become more critical when decisions must be made that affect one's future direction. Yet, "in all this we are more than conquerors through him who loves us" (Rom. 8:37).

Scales of Commitment

The following questions were used in a study by Dean Hoge, John Dybel, and David Polk.[15] They are helpful for reflection concerning where a person now is in her or his life cycle.

Index of Commitment of Present Pastorate

1. How seriously, if at all, have you thought *during the last year* that you would like to leave your present pastorate?

Never thought about it	20 percent
Not at all seriously	31 percent
Somewhat seriously	26 percent
Quite seriously; considering it	13 percent
Very seriously; now trying to leave	10 percent

2. How strong is your commitment to your present pastorate as your proper place of ministry at this time?

Very strong	43 percent
Moderately strong	33 percent
Partly strong, partly weak	16 percent
Quite weak	3 percent
No commitment; ready to change	6 percent

3. In general, would you like to continue in your present pastorate or not

Strongly like to continue	44 percent
Moderately like to continue	23 percent
Partly like to continue, partly like to leave	18 percent
Moderately like to leave	6 percent
Strongly like to leave	8 percent

Index of Commitment to the Ministry

1. How strong is your commitment to the ministry as your vocation?

Very strong	68 percent
Moderately strong	24 percent
Partly strong, partly weak	7 percent
Quite weak	1 percent
No commitment, ready to change	<1 percent

2. Would you enter the ministry again, if you had it to do over?

Definitely yes	58 percent
Probably yes	29 percent
Uncertain	9 percent
Probably no	2 percent
Definitely no	2 percent

3. How certain are you that the ministry is the right profession for you?

Very certain	58 percent
Moderately certain	31 percent
Partly certain, partly uncertain	9 percent
Moderately uncertain	1 percent
Very uncertain	1 percent

4. How seriously, if at all, have you thought *during the last year* about leaving the ministry?

Never thought about it	28 percent
Not at all seriously	45 percent
Somewhat seriously	19 percent
Quite seriously, considering it	6 percent
Very seriously; now trying to leave	1 percent

Chapter 12.
Surviving and Surmounting Ministry

Ministry can be survived as well as surmounted. The case of Brother Dan, a minister in a small southern town in the late 1950s, illustrates this thought.

> "I understand there has been a lot of racial unrest in this area. Is it true that the minister of First Congregational Church is in favor of integration of Negroes with whites?"
>
> "That's correct. Many of us believe he's a Communist. He acts like a Yankee who doesn't know what it's like around here. We treat our Negroes well. It would be wrong to integrate the races. I write an editorial against him every time he preaches about race relations—and that is about every week! I keep track with what he says. He preaches at my church."
>
> "Then, why don't you have him fired?" queries the reporter.
>
> "Fire him? Never!" the editor replies. "He's my pastor. Why, the night my mother died he was the first one to come to the house and the last one to leave."

What makes this story remarkable is the fact that Brother Dan, as people affectionately knew him, had pastored this particular church for eleven years in an era when ministers in the denomination in which he served usually stayed at their churches, on the average, less than four years.

Brother Dan had learned to survive in ministry while taking a highly visible, but unpopular, prophetic stance regarding race relations. He was a very, very good *pastor*. The people knew it, and the community knew it. He cared *about* and *for* people.

Ministry is full of misery as well as grandeur. Learning how to survive the tough times is a skill that can be learned and practiced. It is tragic when otherwise able people leave the ministry because they do not possess these tools for surviving and surmounting.

Before describing some of these skills, the difference between survival and surmounting should be stated. *Survival* means to make it through the storm; make it to the end of a race; not give in to pressure; endure; outlast one's opponents.

People do not want just to survive, however. They want to surmount. *Surmount* means to succeed in spite of; rise above the storm; overcome resistance; transcend the difficulties.

In a sense, learning how to survive includes learning how to surmount. Both are intricately bound together. Brother Dan's eleven years as a pastor in a very challenging situation entailed more than survival. In important ways, he had surmounted. People listened even though they did not always agree with his convictions. He carried on a prophetic, as well as a pastoral, ministry. He felt fulfilled in what he did. He was surmounting. If asked, we are sure he would have stated his preference for not filling any other role than being a clergyperson in that church and at that time.

Although surviving and surmounting are not radically different, keeping the distinctiveness in mind is important. Nevertheless, we recognize such differences may be more artificial than real. Cultivating the following skills will enable any pastor to do a better job of surviving and surmounting ministry: (1) specialize, (2) negotiate, (3) change intentionally, and (4) engage in career development.

Specialize

Brother Dan specialized. He was good at "pastoring," and he specialized in it.

In chapter 3, "What Clergy Do with Their Time," we described the Inventory of Religious Activities and Interests, which lists ten roles that parish clergy play. These include pastoral counseling, administration, Christian education, preaching, spiritual guidance, worship leadership, and social action, among others.

No minister can do all these tasks exceptionally well—if only because a pastor does not have adequate time to develop proficiency in each one. More importantly, although parish clergy are "generalists" and churches expect them to function in each of these roles, it is a very rare minister who enjoys them all or can perform equally well in all of them.

A strategic way of surviving is to determine in which of the roles one excels and to specialize in it. Although parishioners would like clergy to excel in every role, their best judgment knows this is impossible, and they tolerate less than optimal performance in some areas if their minister does one or more of them exceptionally well. Most clergy do some things well. To discover these and emphasize them is the skill of "specialization."

In his "idiosyncrasy credit" theory of leadership, social psychologist Edwin Hollander describes the way specializing helps clergy survive. He suggests that effective leaders do two things for groups. First, they help groups do better in what they are already doing, and second, they help groups do what they are not, but should be, doing. Since leaders cannot be leaders without followers, Hollander states that people follow leaders more easily in doing what they are already doing than in doing something new—even if it is what they should be doing![1]

Groups learn to trust and support leaders who help them do more effectively what they already do. In the case of churches, everyone assumes the church will engage in worship, teaching, evangelizing, and pastoral care. Brother Dan evoked trust and support by excelling in the pastoral role. Hollander believes that leaders who emphasize one of these *expected* roles build up the credit (i.e., support and trust) needed to lead the group into new areas. In the church, this often means the "prophetic" role. Brother Dan gained support of the newspaper editor to speak out regarding race relations because of the credit he had built from being a good and caring pastor.

We are convinced that specializing works. It is almost unheard of for ministers to have the "hoof and mouth disease." This is the disease of inadequacy in all areas, the disease of those who "can't preach and won't visit," as one old-timer put it. Almost all ministers have one or more areas of *expected* ministry in which they are exceptionally good. Determining those roles and specializing in them will give clergy the credit they need to survive the hard times during which people do not agree with them.[2]

The opposite of specializing is "generalizing." As noted in chapter 3, parish ministers expect to work in many areas of ministry each week and to do them well. "Generalizing" is an occupational hazard of pastoring a church. Not only will specializing earn credit for ministers among their parishioners, it will also help to keep clergy from burnout. Boyd states it well when he notes that "excessive demands invariably accompany a clerical career."[3]

He cites several studies reinforcing this widely acknowledged contention that the demands of clergy are overwhelming. He reports the conclusion of the Bishops' Committee on Priestly Life and Ministry (1982): "The sheer increase of demands on a priest's time, many of which need his immediate attention, has produced a

new dimension of urgency in his work."[4] A survey by the Ministers'
and Casualty Union found that one-half of all clergy work more
than 10 hours per day.[5] And a study for the executive council of
the Episcopal Church found that the average work week for parish
priests was 66.7 hours.[6] Not surprisingly, over-extension is the
primary complaint of pastors seeking help at the Menninger
Foundation; there are too many commitments for their time and
energy.[7]

In order to specialize successfully, rather than generalize, it is
often wise to "negotiate," which is the second skill for surviving
and surmounting in ministry.

Negotiate

We are not sure if Brother Dan had a clear understanding with
his church that allowed him to "specialize" in pastoral care, but we
are convinced he would have been appreciated even more if he
did. The process whereby such clear agreements are reached is
known as "negotiating a ministry."[8]

Almost every church has a personnel committee that supposedly
deals with the tasks parishioners expect clergy to do. One of the
better names we have heard for such a committee is the "Pastor-
Parish Relations Committee." This title clearly indicates that the
committee's function is to relate the pastor to the parish in the
best possible way.

Since no pastor does all things well, the prime task of this committee should be to assist in determining the kinds of ministries
the pastor does best and communicate these to the parish.
Furthermore, this committee should delegate certain clergy roles
to other staff and laypersons who do them better and/or help
lower expectations of the parish in those areas where a given
minister does not function as well as in others.

"Negotiating" becomes a tool for survival at this point. In a study
of burned-out executives, Carver found that most executives lasted
less than two years and those who stayed longer had clear job
contracts that relieved stress and ambiguity.[9] One might think of
clergy as the "chief executive officers" of their parishes. Far too
often, clergy accept their positions without any clearly defined job
descriptions. When this occurs, it is more the fault of the minister
than the parish.

We believe strongly that those clergy who want to survive and
surmount in ministry will negotiate their roles when they begin
work in a parish and again at those times when their interests and
abilities change. The Alban Institute, a consulting service for

parishes, sponsored by the Episcopal Church, recommends that churches employ a consultant to assist them during the first eighteen months after a new priest arrives in the parish. Without doubt, the resulting collaborative negotiations increase the likelihood that clergy will be able to survive.

Periodic renegotiations are probably even more important than the initial negotiation that should take place when the minister first comes to a parish. Over the life span of a career, clergy interests change. For example, many ministers enjoy working with youth early in their careers. As they grow older and their energies wane, they may want to focus on a different area. At one time, a minister may have strong interest in liturgy, while later this same pastor may find spiritual direction more rewarding.

Acknowledging that interests fluctuate from time to time is realistic and very important. Clergy roles should be renegotiated to keep ministry alive and fulfilling. It is no "crime" to say one prefers teaching the Bible to serving a year as an officer in the ministerial association. After all, humdrum and boredom exist—even in ministry!

One should keep in mind the difference between *interests* and *abilities*. Brother Dan had an ability to do pastoral work. We do not know if he had an interest in it. *Interests* are those activities that people enjoy doing and to which they are attracted. *Abilities* are those activities that people do well even if they do not like doing them. The ideal ministerial situation occurs when interests and abilities are identical. Unfortunately, too often this is not the case.

One minister with whom we consulted illustrated these differences between interests and abilities. After taking the Inventory of Religious Activities and Interests, he noted that he rated below average on the role of pastoral counseling. He commented, "The test asked what I enjoy doing. I don't particularly like to counsel. I guess I'm below average in my interest in that area; however," he continued, "if the test had asked what I'm good at doing I would have rated much higher. I'm a good counselor." We asked if he spent much time doing pastoral counseling. "Oh, yes," he replied. "My people expect me to be available for them when they need me. I spend a lot of time counseling."

This pastor had counseling "ability" but little counseling "interest." He spent significant time counseling, however, because his parishioners expected this. Perhaps he had "negotiated" an agreement with his Pastor-Parish Relations Committee to give extra time to counseling in order to feel free to develop aspects of ministry in which he had stronger interest.

"Negotiating a ministry" is a crucial skill for surviving and surmounting. Note one caution, however. Since parish ministry always
takes place in a "church" setting, remember that ministry is vulnerable to the inherent difficulties encountered when leading *any*
voluntary organization. The church has been labeled "a disorgan-
ized organization or an organized disorganization" in that the best
laid plans are always susceptible to individual, subjective sabotage.[10]

No negotiated ministry will please all the people regardless of
how well the Pastor-Parish Relations Committee has communicated the plan to the church. Even negotiated ministries last only
for a time. A congregation's expectations change as much as the
interests of clergy. While negotiation is a valuable tool, it should
never be thought of as a cure-all for surviving and surmounting.

Negotiating the various pastoral ministries enables one to work
with more energy and effectiveness, but negotiating needs to be
intermixed with *intentional change*. This is the next skill we recommend.

Intentional Change

Negotiating could be conceived as "fitting the job to the person." *Intentional change* could be conceived as "fitting the person
to the job." For ministry to function in effective and fulfilling ways
over a lifetime, a pastor will spend time developing skills in both.

The pastor who noted that his scores on the Inventory of
Religious Activities and Interests would differ depending on
whether they measured interests, abilities, or job demands illustrated three of the four components of clergy effectiveness. The
only component omitted was "destiny"—the perception that one
does what Almighty God has called him or her to do. If a person
feels "called" to do what he or she is interested in doing, if this is
what others expect, and if one does this well, maximum effectiveness will result. This is the best of all possible worlds.

Intentional change refers to this area of what one does well—
one's abilities. In ministry, there are two common thoughts about
abilities: (1) ability to be a minister is a gift, or innate talent, and
(2) the skills of ministry are taught and refined in seminary. Both of
these are wrong.

While it may be true that character traits such as extroverted-
ness and interpersonal sensitivity are preferred in a ministerial
vocation, most clergy would agree that effectiveness is not "born"
but made. Those who depend on natural talents alone do not last
long, and they seldom find lasting fulfillment.

Concerning the place for learning the skills of ministry (i.e., seminary), Jud, Mills, and Burch spoke for many when they observed, "Young people choose the ministry with one set of ideals and occupational images, they are introduced to a radically different set in the seminaries, and when they emerge as neophyte ministers into local parishes they discover additional roles and obligations for which they were never trained."[11] Perhaps what seminarians learn is a scholarly model somewhat irrelevant to the collaborative, administrative, relational skills that make up the essence of ministry in the local parish.[12]

The prime place for learning about the skills of ministry is the parish itself. And the prime time for acquiring new abilities is *after* seminary training while one works in a parish situation. We have taught both seminary students and clergy involved in the pastorate while pursuing the doctor of ministry degree. In far too many cases, the seminary students don't even know the appropriate questions to ask. Without exception, the most highly motivated and most easily trained students are active clergy. They are eager to learn new abilities and refine the skills they have.

Pastors who are actively engaged in daily responsibilities of a church know they need to do *better*. They have learned what effective ministry requires. And they realize that there is no better time than the present to acquire these abilities. Having experienced ministry from the inside, they have no doubt, in the least, that adults can "intentionally change" for the better. They know that "old dogs *can* learn new tricks."

Developing the skill of intentionally changing throughout one's career is a valuable asset in the struggle of surviving and surmounting ministry. This commitment to regular change can have significant effect on what clergy do and how they do it. One can change both content and style. Only those who give up on themselves become so set in their ways that they cannot respond to new insight and training.

Feedback is the key to intentional change. While much can be said for self-evaluation, and while most clergy know more about their performance than they admit, some well-known psychodynamic processes militate against full self-awareness. Add to this truth the fact that ministry is an interactive role in which one continually needs to ask parishioners, How do you like the service you are receiving? Then one can begin to understand the importance of honest feedback.

Those clergy who survive and surmount ministry successfully obtain and use feedback. It is likely that the vast majority of clergy limit their feedback to comments they receive at the door of the church after weekly worship services. In most such cases, they are looking for approval rather than a fair critique of performance. Few leaders in industry would limit themselves to such informal feedback.

Formal, regular, balanced, and all-encompassing evaluations of clergy performance are needed. Only when this happens can congregations expect ministers to do what mature adults can uniquely do, namely, "intentionally change." This does not mean that clergy should become chameleons—changing with every reaction, good or bad. It does mean that clergy should recognize clearly the necessity to evoke positive response from their parishioners if they are to survive. They must never forget that churches are voluntary organizations where people express approval with their presence and their money. Hearing and accepting feedback and intentionally changing also mean that ministers strongly desire to increase their effectiveness.

We stated that evaluation should be "formal," "regular," and "all-encompassing." By this we mean that clergy should not depend exclusively on anecdotal remarks made by parishioners in casual situations. Procedures should be designed, agreed upon, publicized, and systematically applied to every area of clergy leadership. Committee chairing as well as sermons; hospital visiting as well as eucharistic celebrations; parties as well as funerals—*all* areas should be evaluated. Methods should be designed by the church officers and reports made to all parishioners. Descriptions of the variety of ways to evaluate clergy are available in such volumes as *Church Organization Development: Perspectives and Processes.*[13]

"Balanced" evaluation means every evaluation should include a section on commendations as well as recommendations. The good intentions of clergy should be acknowledged and affirmed. Probably no clergyperson's performance in any one of their varied ministerial roles is all bad. An individual can accomplish intentional change to a greater extent if he or she has a foundation of basic affirmation. For example, it is one thing for priests to change the length of sermons when engaged in collaboration with parishioners to improve the worship services and thereby attract more people to attend. It is quite another thing for priests to shorten sermons when told that ten families are so disenchanted they may leave. Clergy change best when not under threat. The balancing of the positive and negative in evaluations is one key to making change possible.

Change, in response to evaluation, can occur in two ways: in *substance* (i.e., what is done) and in *style* (i.e., how it is done). For example, if parishioners report they like their pastor but do not feel spiritually fed by her or his sermons, they are referring to substance. If they report, however, that hospital visits are abrupt and hurried, even though their pastor never fails to call, they are referring to style.

Clergy who want to survive and surmount need to commit themselves to intentional change in *both* substance and style. Becoming predictable, unresponsive, and "set in one's ways" are not the inevitable results of growing up and growing old. These characteristics develop only in those who choose not to make intentional changes along life's way. Clergy need to remain malleable and willing to change. One way this can take place in a feasible way is through career development—the next key to surviving and surmounting in ministry.

Career Development

One of the prime ways to survive and surmount ministry is through career development. In understanding career development, it is important to distinguish between "a career" and "a job." A career is a lifelong commitment to a given occupation; a job is the particular position one holds at a given time and place. Most clergy have one career but several jobs throughout their lives.

Career development is a means for being effective and fulfilled in ministry. It is not necessarily a way to always succeed in a given job. In fact, clergy may find that they self-consciously give up one job for another in order to better express their career of ministry. Some pastors may move from California to Ohio because they feel "the call of God," while others may change positions for more mundane reasons such as a raise in salary. Of course, sometimes parishes relieve clergy of their positions. Especially at these times, it is wise and helpful to keep the distinction between career and job in mind. Clergy may not function successfully in one position but be very effective in another. The loss of a job does not mean the end of a career.

By participating in career development on a regular basis, clergy can keep up with major developments in ministry, learn new skills in management and other areas, reflect with other clergy about common problems and possibilities, acquire skills for personal and family development, and forestall burnout. Many denominations allow regular times during a year for study leave. Clergy should take advantage of every day they are allowed, if only to get out of the parish for meditation at a nearby retreat center.

The first, and perhaps primary, area for career development is personal piety. It is no accident that the word for clergy on the American frontier was *parson*. The term derived from the fact that the minister lived in a house provided by the church—the parsonage—and thereby represented the *church* and *God* in the community. As Rediger noted, "There is a role mystique which suggests pastors should have an infinite capacity to work and suffer and still bounce back and be solid models of Christian leadership. . . . Pastors are the identified leaders of society's chief moral-valuing institution. As such, they are expected to model perfection, to have all the answers to moral questions. . . ."[14]

Interestingly, the word *piety* has fallen into disrepute in Western society. We seem to have become an activist culture in which genuine spirituality is not valued. The characteristics of successful ministers on the Strong Campbell Vocational Interest Blank do not include a "pious" dimension.

This overt deemphasis on the spiritual characteristics of clergy may be more apparent than real, however. As Rediger noted, parishioners still look to their clergy for "moral valuing," both in their personal and professional lives. As one parishioner reportedly said to Phillips Brooks before a Sunday service, "Do you have a fresh message from God for us this morning, pastor?" Many, if not most, parishioners still have that hope. This is borne out in the results of the Readiness for Ministry Study: one of the six major expectations parishioners have of clergy is that they will "be theologians in life and thought."[15]

The development of the spiritual life is one facet of ministry to which clergy—Protestant as well as Roman Catholic—must *consciously* attend, or it will not get done. One does not become spiritually mature by osmosis. It is not easy to be genuinely spiritual in twentieth-century culture. The activist, materialist temptation is great. Cultivating piety should be a major focus of clergy career development. Learning the skills of discipline, study, meditation, and prayer requires intentionality. And this is not a talent or a gift that comes without effort.

The second area of career development considered important for those interested in successfully surviving and surmounting ministry is management skills. If there is one area for which clergy routinely report they are underprepared, it is in the area of managing the church. We intentionally use the word *management* instead of *leadership*. While the roles of vision and inspiration are valuable and integral to leadership, they are distinctly different from the roles of coordinating and executing, which are the tasks of management. Because clergy report they lack these skills, learning how to manage becomes a very important part of post-seminary career development.

Perhaps this is the best way for clergy to grow into maximum effectiveness in the church. When they begin ministry, most pastors are inspired by the vision of the call of God through the gospel message. They are less convinced that Christian faith is synonymous with the Christian church. As noted earlier, James Dittes concluded in his perceptive volume *The Church in the Way* that for many clergy the church does, in fact, get *in the way* of the Christian gospel.[16] After accepting a call and experiencing what "pastoring" is all about, they discover two things. First, there is no way around involvement with the church. Since they have chosen ministry as a vocation, the only way to make a living in a parish situation is to work in a church that pays them. Second, resistances to their ideas from parishioners are but the latest expressions of recalcitrance, seen in God's people from the call of Abraham, to the Exodus, to the Davidic monarchy, to the building of the Temple, to the establishment of the synagogue, to the messages of the prophets, to the founding of the New Testament church. Clergy become aware of a theology of the church that suggests that Jewish/Christian faith and the church are one. The local church is an essential not an elective.

Thus, managing the church is not an option. It is a necessity. And management is not an innate gift. It is skill that can be learned. The church—like any voluntary organization—can be managed well, but the task is one that can be taught rather than caught! Clergy should not be embarrassed to say, "I need to learn to manage." If they want to successfully survive and surmount in ministry, they will make management training an integral part of their career development.

The last aspect of career development considered important is personal growth. This is not the same as spiritual development discussed earlier. Personal growth refers to such "off the job" issues as relaxation training, marriage enrichment, and burnout prevention.

A Gallup poll in 1983 reported that nearly one of every three ministers had often or occasionally considered leaving the ministry because of the frustrations experienced in the role. There is no question but that clergy, along with all those in the helping professions, have often come near to burnout, defined as "the emotional exhaustion resulting from the stress of interpersonal contact . . . in which helping professionals lose positive feelings, sympathy, and respect for their clients."[17]

But stress does not need to lead to burnout. *Christianity Today* reported the finding of Harvard psychiatrist George Vailant that stress had little effect on the forty-year follow-up of the lives of ninety-five healthy young men. "What was important," said Dr. Vailant, "was how they responded to stress."[18] Appropriate reaction to stress is a skill that can be learned through intentional career development. Clergy who want to survive and surmount in ministry should include this type of training in their lives.

Deep muscle relaxation is a set of procedures one can learn through continuing education programs of many community colleges or from numerous counselors and biofeedback practitioners. Learning to recognize such processes as the "post-adrenaline blues"—common to clergy on Mondays after stimulating activity on Sundays—can be obtained through reading such self-help books as Archibald Hart's *Coping with Depression in Ministry and Other Helping Professions*.[19]

Developing extraministerial avocations or hobbies is another skill among the many that constitute burnout prevention efforts. We are acquainted with stamp collectors, golfers, old-car restorers, and bridge players—all clergypersons who have decided not to take ministry so seriously that they do nothing else. We know a minister who secludes himself in a back bedroom every Friday. Here he spends a minimum of four hours playing with model trains. These hobbies may be ways clergy have of taking ministry "so seriously" that they refuse to burnout before their time is up!

A final aspect of personal growth, which we reemphasize, is marriage enrichment. We noted the importance of continuing to attend to marriage relationships in chapter 6, "The Minister's Love Life." It is worth mentioning again. One of the tragedies—seemingly endemic to executive-type positions—is that people often neglect their marriage relationship. Not surprisingly, the result is deterioration. This is especially tragic in ministry.

Intimate relationships are essential to personhood. Marriage degenerates into an arrangement over time if not intentionally cultivated. Because people erroneously assume that clergy marriages, like clergypersons, are perfect and without difficulties, it is especially hard for ministers to engage publically in activities that enrich marriage. The payoff, however, is great if clergy couples actively make their relationship a self-conscious part of their personal growth. We mean more than making time for one another. We feel that intentional study of the dynamics of the experience of intimacy, open dialogue about changing expressions of affection, and attendance at meetings where marriage is the topic of concern are important means for achieving fulfilling marriage.

Conclusion

This chapter has considered a variety of prescriptions for surviving and surmounting ministry. We have discussed not only longevity but fulfillment; not only holding on to a job but finding lifelong fulfillment in a career. We began this chapter with the story of Brother Dan, who had learned to survive. Knowing him well, we are convinced that he had also learned to surmount and to find great satisfaction in being prophet as well as priest. Although he did not have the benefit of this chapter, we feel sure he did many of these things intuitively. While our prescriptions are not exhaustive, by any means, we are convinced that clergy will not go wrong in applying them to their professional lives.

Notes

Introduction

1. Erik Erikson, *Childhood and Society*, 2d ed. (New York: W.W. Norton, 1963), 268.

Chapter 1. Ministry: A Unique Position

1. E. Brooks Holifield, "The Hero and the Minister in American Culture," *Theology Today* 33 (1977): 337-79.

2. Jackson W. Carroll, "Some Issues in Clergy Authority," *Review of Religious Research* 23 (1981): 99-117.

3. Ibid., 99-117.

4. Thomas M. Gannon, S.J., "Priest Minister: Profession or Non-profession," *Review of Religious Research* 12 (1971): 66-79.

5. Ibid., 67.

Chapter 2. Why People Enter Ministry

1. Erik Erikson, *Young Man Luther* (New York: W.W. Norton, 1958).

2. Allen Nauss, "The Ministerial Personality: Myth or Reality," *Journal of Religion and Health* 12 (1973): 77-95.

3. Katherine C. Briggs and Isabel B. Myers, "Myers-Briggs Type Inventory Form F" (Palo Alto, Calif.: Counseling Psychologists Press, 1976).

4. B.N. Ekhardt and W.M. Goldsmith, "Personality Factors of Men and Women Pastoral Candidates," *Journal of Psychology and Theology* 12 (1984): 109-18.

5. C.W. Ellison and W.S. Mattila, "The Needs of Evangelical Christian Leaders in the United States," *Journal of Psychology and Theology* 11 (1985): 28-35.

6. R.J. Menges and James E. Dittes, *Psychological Studies of Clergymen: Abstracts of Research* (New York: Thomas Nelson and Sons, 1965).

7. J.J. Fabry, "An Extended Concurrent Validation of the Vocational Preferences of Clergymen," *Psychological Reports* 26 (1975): 947-50.

8. Sam C. Webb, *An Inventory of Religious Activities and Interests* (Princeton, N.J.: Educational Testing Service, 1967).

9. James E. Dittes, *Minister on the Spot.* (Philadelphia: Pilgrim Press, 1970).

10. C.W. Christensen, "The Role of a Psychiatric Consultant to a Theological Seminary," *Journal of Pastoral Care* 9 (1955): 1-7.

11. Anton T. Boisen, "Psychiatric Screening of Theological Students (reply to C.W. Christensen)," *Journal of Pastoral Care* 9 (1955): 166.

12. Ministry Studies Board, "Theological School Inventory" (Dallas: Ministry Inventories, 1972).

Chapter 3. What Clergy Do with Their Time

1. Mark May, *The Education of American Ministers* (New York: Institute of Social and Religious Research, 1934). Also see David S. Schuller, Merton P. Strommen, and Milo L. Brekke, eds., *Ministry in America* (New York: Harper & Row, 1980), especially Daniel O. Aleshire, "Eleven Major Areas of Ministry," 23-53.

2. Samuel Blizzard, "The Minister's Dilemma," *Christian Century* 17 (1956): 508-10, and "The Parish Minister's Self-Image of His Master Role," *Pastoral Psychology* 89 (1958): 25.

3. Richard A. Blackmon, "The Hazards of Ministry" (Ph.D. diss. Graduate School of Psychology, Fuller Theological Seminary, 1984), 23.

4. Sam C. Webb, *An Inventory of Religious Activities and Interests* (Princeton, N.J.: Educational Testing Service, 1967).

5. Richard A. Hunt, Sue W. Cardwell, and James E. Dittes, *Manual for the Theological School Inventory, Form D* (Pasadena, CA: Ministry Inventories, 1976). Fred Kling originally conceptualized the structure and initial research on the Theological School Inventory, with cooperation from several researchers. James E. Dittes wrote the first edition of the manual and developed Form C, which was published by Educational Testing Service in 1962. James Ashbrook, Harry DeWire, and Edgar W. Mills, Jr., were

involved in making the TSI available to seminaries. Richard A. Hunt, Sue Webb Cardwell, and James E. Dittes wrote the revised Form D in 1972 and the manual and guide in 1976. In 1990, Hunt, Cardwell, and Daniel O. Aleshire wrote the Form E revision, with consultation from Kling and Dittes.

6. Schuller, Strommen, and Brekke, eds., *Ministry in America*.

7. Merton P. Strommen, "Models of Ministry," in Schuller, Strommen, and Brekke, eds., *Ministry in America*, 54–89.

8. Blackmon, "Hazards of Ministry," 23.

9. Merrill E. Douglas and Joyce McNally, "How Ministers Use Time," *Christian Ministry* 11 (1980): 22–27.

10. Ibid., 25.

11. J. Conrad Glass, "Ministerial Job Satisfaction Scale," *Review of Religious Research* 17 (1976): 153–57.

12. C.L. Rassieur, "Ministry Without Shame," *Christian Ministry* (January 1984): 7–10.

13. James E. Dittes, *Minister on the Spot* (Philadelphia: Pilgrim Press, 1970).

14. Blackmon, "The Hazards of Ministry," 23.

15. David Mace and Vera Mace, *What's Happening to Clergy Marriages?* (Nashville: Abingdon Press, 1980); William Hulme, *Your Pastor's Problems: A Guide for Ministers and Laymen* (Minneapolis: Augsburg, 1966).

16. Blackmon, "The Hazards of Ministry," 23.

17. Roy M. Oswald, *Clergy Stress: A Survival Kit for Church Professionals* (Washington, D.C.: Alban Institute, 1982a); Roy M. Oswald, *Clergy Burnout, A Survival Kit for Church Professionals* (Washington, D.C.: Alban Institute, 1982b).

Chapter 4. The Hazards of Ministry

1. Richard A. Blackmon, "The Hazards of Ministry" (Ph.D. diss. Graduate School of Psychology, Fuller Theological Seminary, 1984), 23.

2. J.C. Holyrod and A.M. Brodsky, "Psychologists' Attitudes and Practices Regarding Erotic and Nonerotic Contact with Patients," *American Psychologist* 32 (1977): 843–49.

3. S.H. Kardener, M. Fuller, and I.N. Mensh, "A Survey of Physicians' Attitudes and Practices Regarding Erotic and Nonerotic Contact with Patients," *American Journal of Psychiatry* 133 (1973): 1324–25.

4. H. Newton Malony, "Dual Role Problems among Psychologists-Clergy" (Paper presented at the annual meeting of the American Psychological Association, Los Angeles, Calif., 1985).

5. H. Newton Malony, T.A. Needham, and S. Southard, *Clergy Malpractice* (Philadelphia: Westminster Press, 1985).

6. Blackmon, "The Hazards of Ministry," 23.

7. G. Jud, E.W. Mills, and G. Burch, *Ex-Pastors: Why Men Leave Parish Ministry*. (Philadelphia: Pilgrim Press, 1970); D. Smith, *Clergy in the Cross Fire: Coping with Role Conflict in Ministry* (Philadelphia: Westminster Press, 1973).

8. Blackmon, "The Hazards of Ministry," 23.

9. Duane P. Alleman, "The Psychological Adjustment of Pastors' Wives" (Ph.D. diss., Graduate School of Psychology, Fuller Theological Seminary, 1987).

10. G.E. Bartlett, "The Minister: Pastor or Promoter?" *Pastoral Psychology* 8 (1957): 15.

11. C.W. Ellison and W. Mattila, "The Needs of Evangelical Christian Leaders in the United States," *Journal of Psychology and Theology* 11 (1985): 28-35.

12. C.A. Rayburn, L.J. Richmond, L. Rogers, and H.N. Malony, "Men, Women, and Stress in the Clergy" (Symposium presented at the annual meeting of the International Council of Psychologists, Mexico City, 1984). The theoretical basis for the Rayburn et al. study was the Osipow and Spokane model of vocational adjustment, which combines role demands, life stress, and personal resources.

Chapter 5. Women in Ministry

1. Edward C. Lehman, Jr., *Women Clergy: Breaking through Gender Barriers* (New Brunswick, N.J.: Transaction Books, 1985), 139ff, 190.

2. Marvin J. Taylor, ed., *Fact Book on Theological Education: 1980-81* (Vandalia, Ohio: American Association of Theological Schools, 1982) 1-10, 72, 74.

3. Lehman, *Women Clergy*, 139ff, 190.

4. Ibid., 274f.

5. Jackson W. Carroll, Barbara Hargrove, and Adair T. Lummis *Women of the Cloth* (San Francisco: Harper & Row, 1981), 208.

6. Lehman,*Women Clergy*, 139ff, 190.

7. Ibid., 282f.

8. Priscilla Proctor and William Proctor, *Women in the Pulpit: Is God an Equal Opportunity Employer?* (Garden City, N.Y.: Doubleday, 1976).

9. Judith L. Weidman, ed., *Women Ministers: How Women Are Redefining Traditional Roles* (New York: Harper & Row, 1981).

10. Sue W. Cardwell, "Why Women Fail/Succeed in Ministry: Psychological Factors," *Pastoral Psychology* 30 (1982): 153-62.

11. Martha Orrick, "Women in the Ministry: Personality and Background Characteristics of a Group of United Methodist Clergy and Theological Students, *Dissertation Abstracts* 45 (8-B), (1985): 2698.

12. Edwin H. Friedman, *Generation to Generation: Family Process in Church and Synagogue* (New York: Guilford Press, 1985).

13. Lehman, *Women Clergy*, 139ff, 190, 293.

14. Carroll W. Jackson and Robert L. Wilson, *Too Many Pastors? The Clergy Job Market* (New York: Pilgrim Press, 1980).

15. Carroll and Wilson, *Too Many Pastors? The Clergy Job Market*; Carroll, Hargrove, and Lummis, *Women of the Cloth*.

16. Carroll, Hargrove, and Lummis, *Women of the Cloth*.

Chapter 6. The Minister's Love Life

1. Duane Alleman, "Pastors' Wives in the 1980's" (Ph.D. diss. Graduate School of Psychology, Fuller Theological Seminary, 1987).

2. William J. Everett, *Blessed Be the Bond* (Philadelphia: Fortress Press, 1985).

3. Richard A. Blackmon, "The Hazards of Ministry" (Ph.D. diss. Graduate School of Psychology, Fuller Theological Seminary, 1984) 17.

4. Douglas S. Miller, "Ministering to Women in Remarriage to Clergymen," *Dissertation Abstracts International* 45 (11-A), (May 1985), 3385-86.

5. Blackmon, "The Hazards of Ministry," 17.

6. Janelle Warner and John Carter, "Loneliness, Martial Adjustment, and Burnout in Pastoral and Lay Persons," *Journal of Psychology and Theology* 12 (1984): 125-131.

7. Blackmon, "The Hazards of Ministry," 17.

8. Ibid., 122.

Chapter 7. Spouse and Parish

1. William Douglas, *Ministers' Wives* (New York: Harper & Row, 1965).

2. Duane Alleman, "Pastors' Wives in the 1980's" (Ph.D. diss. Graduate School of Psychology, Fuller Theological Seminary, 1987).

3. Ibid., 98.

4. Richard A. Blackmon, "The Hazards of Ministry" (Ph.D. diss. Graduate School of Psychology, Fuller Theological Seminary, 1984).

5. Alleman, "Pastors' Wives in the 1980's."

6. Douglas, *Ministers' Wives*.

7. Alleman, "Pastors' Wives in the 1980's."

8. Ibid., 106.

9. Ibid., 109.

10. Edwin H. Friedman, *Generation to Generation: Family Process in Church and Synagogue* (New York: Guilford Press, 1985).

11. L. Guy Mehl, "Marriage and Ministry in Midlife," *Journal of Religion and Health* 23 (1984): 290–98.

12. Mary Paula Walsh, "Role Conflicts among Women in Ministry," *Dissertation Abstracts* 45 (1984): 1551.

Chapter 8. Dual-Careers in Clergy Life

1. Richard Hunt and Joan A. Hunt, *Ministry and Marriage* (Pasadena, CA: Ministry Inventories, 1977).

2. Francine Hall and Douglas T. Hall, *The Two-Career Couple* (Reading, MS: Addison-Wesley, 1979), 121.

3. Eric Erikson, *Childhood and Society* (New York: W.W. Norton, 1964).

4. Daniel J. Levinson, *The Seasons of a Man's Life* (New York: Knopf, 1978).

5. T.J. Paolino and B.S. McCrady, eds., *Marriage and Marital Therapy: Psychoanalytic, Behavioral, and Systems Theory Perspectives* (New York: Brunner/Mazel, 1978).

6. Neil S. Jacobson and Alan S. Gurman, eds., *Clinical Handbook of Marital Therapy* (New York: Guilford Press, 1986).

7. Edwin H. Friedman, *Generation to Generation: Family Process in Church and Synagogue* (New York: Guilford Press, 1985).

8. Hall and Hall, *Two-Career Couple*, 121.

9. Ibid., 46f.

10. Herbert Lunt Robinson, Jr., "Hazards of the Ministry for Dual-Clergy Couples" (Ph.D. diss. Graduate School of Psychology, Fuller Theological Seminary, 1988).

Chapter 9. Staff Relationships in Ministry

1. C. Miller, "Fiddlin' with the Staff," *Leadership* 7 (1986): 104-8.

2. Norman Shawchuck, "A Candid Letter to Senior Pastors," *Leadership* 1 (1980): 85.

3. Kenneth R. Mitchell, *Psychological and Theological Relationships in the Multiple Staff Ministry* (Philadelphia: Westminster, 1967), 13.

4. Shawchuck, "Candid Letter," 85.

5. Shawchuck, "Candid Letter," 85.

6. Mitchell, *Psychological and Theological Relationships*, 170.

7. Ibid., 164.

8. Shawchuck, "Candid Letter," 87.

9. Mitchell, *Psychological and Theological Relationships*, 38.

10. L. Kageler, "Performance Reviews: Worth the Trouble?" *Leadership* 6 (1985): 24-30.

11. Mitchell, *Psychological and Theological Relationships*. 237-8.

Chapter 10. Ministerial Effectiveness

1. J. Free and H.N. Malony, "The Incorporating Body: How Churches Gain and Hold Members" (Paper presented at the annual meeting of the Religious Research Association, Chicago, 1978).

2. Richard Wilke, *And Are We Yet Alive?* (Nashville, Tenn. Abingdon, 1986).

3. Free and Malony, "Incorporating Body."

4. Allen Nauss, "Seven Profiles of Effective Ministers," *Review of Religious Research* 24 (1983): 334-46.

5. H.N. Malony, "Ministerial Effectiveness: A Review of Recent Research," *Pastoral Psychology* 33 (1984): 96-104.

6. H.N. Malony, "The Clinical Assessment of Optimal Religious Functioning," *Review of Religious Research* 30 (1988): 3-17.

7. Ibid., 14.

8. Ibid., 14.

9. Ibid., 4.

10. H.N. Malony, *Church Organization Development: Perspectives and Processes* (Pasadena, Calif.: Integration Press, 1986).

11. Gordon Allport and J.M. Ross, "Personal Religious Orientation and Prejudice," *Journal of Personality and Social Psychology* 5 (1967): 432-43.

12. B.R. Howe, "Defining Ministerial Effectiveness in Terms of the Change Effects in the Persons Ministered To" (Ph.D. diss., Graduate School of Psychology, Fuller Theological Seminary, 1980).

13. J.E. Dittes, *The Church in the Way* (New York: Scribners, 1967).

14. H.N. Malony, "Motivation and Management: The M and Ms of the Pastor's Task," In Church Organization Development, 99-107.

Chapter 11. The Life Cycle of Ministry

1. Harbaugh, G.L. and Rogers, E., "Pastoral Burnout: A View from the Seminary," *Journal of Pastoral Care*, 1984, June, 99-106.

2. Richard A. Hunt, James E. Dittes, and Sue Cardwell, *Manual for the Theological School Inventory* (Pasadena, CA: Ministry Inventories, 1976).

3. G. Jud, E.W. Mills, and G. Burch, *Ex-Pastors: Why Men Leave Parish Ministry* (Philadelphia: Pilgrim Press, 1970).

4. Moore, William J., "The Relationship Between Unrealistic Self Expectations and Burnout Among Pastors" (Psy. D. dissertation, Rosemead Graduate School of Psychology, 1984).

5. Edwin H. Friedman, *Generation to Generation: Family Process in Church and Synagogue* (New York: Guilford Press, 1985).

6. Hunt, Dittes, and Cardwell, *Theological School Inventory*.

7. Ibid.

8. Dean R. Hoge, John E. Dybel, and David T. Polk, "Organizational and Situational Influences on Vocational Commitment of Protestant Ministers," *Review of Religious Research*, 23 (December 1981): 133-49.

9. Les L. Steele, "The Adult Development of Protestant Male Clergy: An Investigation of Attitudinal Change in the Adult Years," *Dissertation Abstracts* 45 (4-A), (October 1984): 1078.

10. David K. Switzer, *The Minister as Crisis Counselor*, rev. ed. (Nashville: Abingdon Press, 1986).

11. Thomas W. Taylor, "The Relation among Achievement Motivation, Marital Satisfaction, Job Satisfaction, and Other Selected Variables among Southern Baptist Pastors," *Dissertation Abstracts International*, 45 (8-B), (February 1985): 2675.

12. Richard A. Blackmon, "The Hazards of Ministry" (Ph.D. diss., Graduate School of Psychology, Fuller Theological Seminary, 1984).

13. Jud, Mills, and Burch, *Ex-Pastors.*

14. Richard N. Bolles, *The Three Boxes of Life and How to Get Out of Them* (Berkeley, CA: Ten Speed Press, 1981).

15. Hoge, Dybel, and Polk, "Organizational and Situational Influences."

Chapter 12. Surviving and Surmounting Ministry

1. E.P. Hollander, "Conformity, Status, and Idiosyncrasy Credit," *Psychological Review* 65 (1965): 117-27.

2. *Unsigned editorial,* "Experts Say Clergy Stress Doesn't Have to Result in Burnout," *Christianity Today* (November 9, 1984): 71-72.

3. D.O. Boyd, "Stress Diagnosis and Clerical Careers," *Journal of Pastoral Counseling* 17 (1982): 61-68.

4. Bishops' Committee on Priestly Life and Ministry, *The Priest and Stress* (Washington, D.C.: United States Catholic Conference, 1982).

5. S.B. Leas, *Time Management: A Working Guide for Church Leaders* (Nashville: Abingdon Press, 1978).

6. S.M. Kelly et al., "Who Do Men Say That I Am?" A Report in Identity and the Parish Priest in the Episcopal Church (Executive Council of the Episcopal Church, Strategic Research Services Group, 1970).

7. D.C. Houts, *Your Pastor's Problems: A Guide for Ministers and Laymen* (Minneapolis: Augsburg, 1977).

8. H.N. Malony, "Negotiating a Ministry" (Unpublished manuscript, Graduate School of Psychology, Fuller Theological Seminary, 1982).

9. G.L. Rediger, *Coping with Clergy Burnout* (Valley Forge, PA: Judson Press, 1982), 22-25.

10. H.N. Malony, *Church Organization Development: Perspectives and Processes* (Pasadena, Calif.: Integration Press, 1986).

11. G. Jud, E.W. Mills, and G.W. Burch, *Ex-Pastor: Why Men Leave the Parish Ministry* (Philadelphia: Pilgrim Press, 1970), 93.

12. R. Kemper, *The New Shape of Ministry* (Nashville: Abingdon Press, 1982).

13. Malony, *Church Organization Development.*

14. Rediger, *Coping with Clergy Burnout*, 22-25.

15. D. Schuller, M. Strommen, and M. Brekke, eds., *Ministry in America* (San Francisco: Harper & Row, 1980).

16. J.E. Dittes, *The Church in the Way* (New York: Scribners, 1965).

17. C. Maslach, "Burnout: How People Cope," *Public Welfare* (Spring 1978): 53.

18. Vailant, "Clergy Stress," 71-72.

19. A.D. Hart, *Coping with Depression in Ministry and Other Helping Professions* (Arcadia, Calif.: Cope Publications, 1984).

Index of Subjects

Index of Names

DATE DUE

FEB 2 6 1997			
MAY 0 5 2005			